Speak, Son

A Mother's Memoir

Book and cover design by Dan D Shafer
Cover photo courtesy Chagit & Roger Deitz
Back cover art by Ciaran O'Shea
Printed in the United States of America

ISBN: 978-1-63405-060-9
LIBRARY OF CONGRESS CONTROL NUMBER: 2023935858

Published by Chin Music Press
1501 Pike Place #329
Seattle, Washington 98101
www.chinmusicpress.com

FIRST PRINTING

Speak, Son

A Mother's Memoir

CHAGIT DEITZ

CHIN MUSIC
P R E S S

Contents

Art by Ciaran O'Shea

for Ben

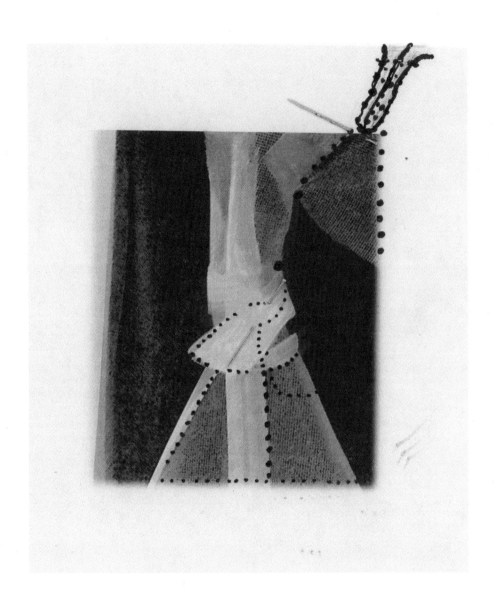

Art by Chagit Deitz

Foreword: Lost one

Penelope sits at her loom, weaving a cloth.
Every night, she will take it apart, unweave it. Like her, I hunch over my
loom, surrounded by my memories of Ben, his writings, photos, books,
and music. I try to interlace it all into a new textile, a "text." Unlike
Penelope, I don't have to unweave it at night. Every thin thread of
my work is priceless, precious, and beloved, and must somehow stay
intact and unharmed. I am witnessing a new entity being born, a
colorful blanket that will keep me warm for the rest of my life.

Benjamin, son of Jacob and Rachel, was the youngest among his
eleven brothers and one sister, Dina. Benjamin, as pronounced in the English
language, is a Hebrew name: Ben-Yamin. Literally translated into English,
Ben Yamin "Son of the right side."

As the Bible story goes, Benjamin's arrival into the world coincides
with his mother's death by childbirth: "And when her labor was at its hardest, the midwife said to her, "Do not fear, for you have another son. And as
her soul was departing (for she was dying), she called his name, Ben-Oni; but
his father called him Benjamin. So, Rachel died, and she was buried on the
way to Ephrath (that is, Bethlehem)" (Genesis 35:17–19). But Jacob did not obey
Rachel's wish to name him Ben-Oni ("son of my sorrow") and named him Ben
Yamin ("son of the right side"). Benjamin would grow up to become the father
of the most powerful tribe of Israel.

We had a son by the same name. But for us, he was always BEN – YAMIN.
Death and sorrow did not cast a shadow over his name. Ben-son we loved

calling you. You were without a doubt a pretty complex guy. From a young age, you were a wind-up toy with boundless energy to live life to the fullest; at the same time, you were fascinated by death and destruction, equally eager to explore the powerful but dark side of life. Extremely intelligent, multi-talented, fast, and curious, you wanted to fly high. Someone who knew you well once remarked to me that in your 32 years of life, you had more experiences than most 80-year-old men. Living life at top speed, changing position and direction of travel as needed, you managed to cover vast amounts of space in a short amount of time.

Your first gray hair appeared when you were only 10 years old.

One day after your tragic death, Roger, your father, my husband, took me for a drive. All of a sudden, he turned to me and said, **"Ben was a true missile. He was launched with full speed into the sky and then he broke into pieces and exploded."** I cannot imagine a better visual metaphor. When we lost you, our hearts shattered as well.

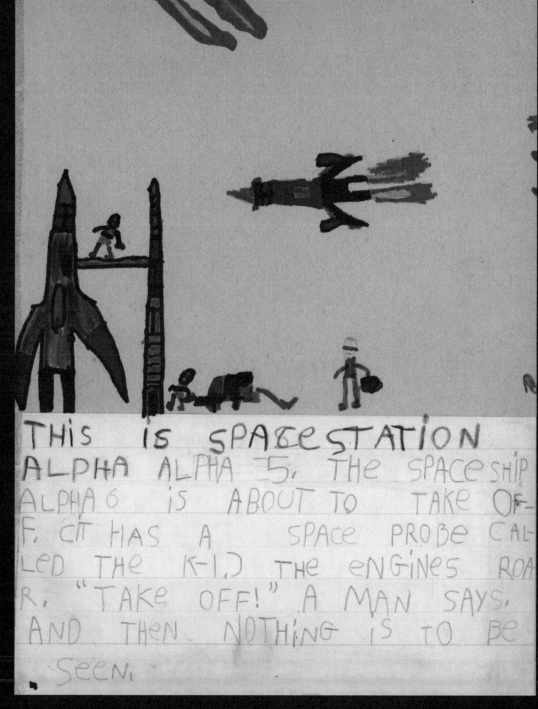

THIS IS SPACE STATION ALPHA ALPHA 5. THE SPACE SHIP ALPHA 6 IS ABOUT TO TAKE OFF. (IT HAS A SPACE PROBE CALLED THE K-1.) THE ENGINES ROAR. "TAKE OFF!" A MAN SAYS. AND THEN NOTHING IS TO BE SEEN.

P'S BOMl BLAMl BLAMl "EEEE-
EEE"l THE COMPUTEP SAYS. THE Kl
SHOOT IT'S OUN BLASTEP'S, BUt THEAT
DEDENT WURK. BOO·O·o·oN!!!

"Space Patrol Part 2: The Enemy Revealed," written and illustrated by Ben Deitz, 5/23/1990

Upon reaching the age of 32, you made the decision to accelerate the speed of your shuttle, traveling far from our center of gravity. We stayed closer to Earth, growing older, safe in the knowledge that one day very soon you will be back with us on Earth. Your stark, silvery-white hair will revert to fine, light brown baby hair, a bit curly and almost covering your eyes. Gazing at us, your arms will reach eagerly forward to hug us. "Welcome back, son," we will say, reaching for you and grabbing on. "We missed you so much," a voice would erupt from inside us. "It is so good to have you back." But I have the feeling that you'll say, "No, I am just here for a moment, checking things out. Don't worry. I found my own way and freedom." And a moment later, in your singularly stylish way, your wings will extend again, ready for another takeoff. At the speed of light, you are off once more to explore life's fancies, always in never-ending, perpetual motion. Just like you exclaimed so poignantly back in the days of rap and middle school.

Ben's Rap (1999)

Change my pitch up
Fill this ditch up
With my rhymes flowin' like kitchup
On ya fries make ya close ya eyes
Wit' surprise
I 'm tired of all ya lies
Cries and alibis
Preyare to downsized
By a barrage of lyrical fury
Cus I ain't in da mood to hurry
Gotcha in my sights
I can see da whites
Of ya peepers startin' ta bring this sound deeper
Cus you da waskelly wabbit
And I'm elmer fudd on speed
So this call you must heed
Folowin' as I lead?
Cause I ain't the type to hit and run
Can'tcha see / that ya time is done
And while it was fun
Put it to your head
And burst it
But firstly, let me reiterate
As my rhymes begin to sedate and create

A false sense of security
Purity sincerity my creativity
Killing you softly wit my song
Soundin' like a gong
Do ya even know what it feels like
To realize your entire life has been wrong?
Flowed from my core on out
Times it gets hard to breathe but I have no doubt
A light will shine upon me from above
Illuminate like love
but I'm getting off the—topic
so let me add to the mix as
I am up my bag of trix
Come getcha lyrical fix
Cus I'm da rhyme pusher on da corner
You come too close
I turn ya family into mourners
The problem is you're too late
So let me educate, medicate and
Reanimate you
Before I express my distress on your
Short-lived state or wellness
Cus I am a cannibal with a hunger
These brutal rhymes rollin' from my tongue like thunder
Cus I am da hammer, you da nail
You da convict, I da jail
I da hurter, you da prey

Ben's Rap '99

change my pitch up
fill this ditch up
with my rhymes flowin' like kitchup
on ~~your~~ ya fries make ya close ya eyes
~~cos ya retch up~~
wit' surprise
I'm tired of all ya lies
cries and alibis
Prepare to be downsized
by ~~a~~ barrage of lyrical fury
~~Bad~~ cus I aint inda mood ta hurry
~~Size yo up in my radar~~
~~You wont get far~~
gotcha in my sights
I can see da whites
of ya ~~eyes~~ peepers startin ta bring this sound deeper
~~double barrel side by side~~
~~you may run but you cant hide~~
cus you da waskelly wabbit
and I'm elmer fudd on speed
~~so heed the call~~ so this call you must heed
followin as I lead?
~~You think~~ you can evade me?

Observing Ben's life from beginning to end causes me emotional pain that is impossible to convey in words. But, in an almost morbid way, this mental undertaking allows me to connect all the chapters of his life. From the past to the present, and forward into the illusionary future.

As I travel on this new journey, exploring and sifting through your writing, I trace your voyage from its beginning. You were a highly sensitive child, one who was unwilling to take certain emotional risks but who simultaneously sought out the most dangerous forms of stimulation, unaware that you were naive and pure—and often ignoring the costs.

I found this in his diary, marked 12-23-96. He was only 13 years old:

"One day while I was buying movie ticket I realized I was counted as an adult. And that for the rest of my life until I am lying dead in my grave I will be counted as an adult. Sure once I reach a certain age I will get senior discount rates, but I will still be an adult. **I will never be able to be a child again. I don't know why, but this thought is pretty unsettling.** Maybe because I didn't live childhood to the fullest. I guess when you think about something that is in plain view and is accepted as truth but never mulled over, the results can be rather unsettling."

My replaying of Ben's life does not offer a straight, elongated vista. It does not follow a linear sequence of events. It is an attempt to free an emotional voyage from its hidden prison and place it gracefully in a new home. I will attempt a furtive butterfly stroke through the waters of his music, reading, writing, his sense of style and humor, his endless love of art and loyalties to friends, all comingled with depression, addiction, and ennui.

Ennui consumed you, it seems. Living in a marginal area in Brooklyn ultimately proved a detriment to your survival; your writing demonstrated insight into the changing way of life in NYC, a knowledge that must have haunted you:

> "I've lived in this city my entire life, and most days, it feels more than ever like it's falling apart. Shiny new condos seem to flower out of the bones of the dying homeless. The serfs wait for overcrowded trains to shuttle them into castle Manhattan where the Lords and Ladies live unaware of the abyss widening beneath them. Police are killing us, and we're killing ourselves, too. The homeless population is, according to my eyes, worse than I've ever witnessed it. The subways are our sewers. Industrial-grade sandpaper is grinding the character of the city into a blunt, uniform white mass for the tourist board to show off. We are living in a fake city, made out of cardboard and paste, hiding a tidal wave of shit behind it.
>
> This how I've been feeling in the past year about this place. I don't mean to be poetic about it, because there's nothing poetic about decay and misery and economic disparity on a level that boggles the mind. **What I'm trying to say is that most days, the magic is gone.** This place is actively hurting people. I used to love the city and now I feel like I'm watching it die and take as many people as it can with it."

Written in April 2015, this was Ben's last Facebook post, a month before his life was taken from him. I did not realize how deeply these views had embedded themselves in his heart. My views were so similar to his, but I preferred to continue wearing my silk blouses, while he chose to live in a building with no elevator and with a leaky bathtub.

Ode to my inability

You are in the ninth grade and do not like your biology teacher. I think that you made her a bit upset by causing some minor disruption during class, likely by not paying attention. You were always busy sketching imaginary figures and robots in your biology notebook. They had very little to do with the structure of the cell, DNA or the creation of proteins. Homework was a distant concept to you, a distraction you did not bother with, and I can imagine your teacher's frustration. She was young and eager to succeed. Just before the final exam, the teacher glanced toward you and remarked: "There is no chance that you will pass, so don't even try."

How little she knew about her student!

We went to Maine for a short vacation around that time, and I noticed that your head was always buried in a book. That wasn't unusual for such an avid reader. The only difference was that for once your head was buried in your biology textbook. It was probably the first time you had even peeked inside it. Unable to grasp the full situation, I did not say a word.

When you received 97 on the exam, I was extremely "proud of you," as I complimented you back then. You looked at me so nonchalantly and answered, "I don't really care about the grade. I only wanted to prove that I can beat the system."

"That's my boy," I whispered to myself. There was no gray area for you. It was always all the way, black and white—from crawling to running with no hesitant small steps, from one glass of wine to the full bottle.

I can't do it
Not like that
No
I thought maybe
Nah
I don't know
I'm
You know
Specific
Got blinds on my periphery, you know?
So, no maybe I might but
I'm not goanna chanciest

HERE, IN HEAVEN

GOITIA DEITZ REMIX

i thought about hanging myself again
but i don't have any rope
and i don't have anything to tie it to
i keep thinking about how they'd find me
having defecated myself
i suppose i'd have to have an enema

Here, in heaven

On May 9, 2015, we went to your apartment in Brooklyn. It was a Saturday. We had seen you last on Thursday night. You hadn't been feeling well, so I cooked your favorite dishes, and your dad and I delivered them to your place. Before we left to go home, you grabbed me and gave me the biggest hug ever. This was unusual for you. After we didn't hear from you for a day and a half, I felt something was not right. We rushed back to your place, though in my heart, I believe I already knew you were gone. The door was locked, and it was dark; the building superintendent managed to open the door, and you were in bed, sleeping like an angel. Your white hair and pale skin created a serene picture. I touched your very cold skin, and a primordial voice that generated from my gut cried out, "He is at peace."

Your white hair and pale skin was covered gently with a black blanket; it was the calmest I had seen you since you were a little baby, resting quietly in your crib. For the first time in so long, you were no longer wandering the tormented regions of your mind. Roger was the first to touch your cold body. "He is gone" was all that he said then. A few moments or seconds later, (who remembers?) I heard him say in a loud, clear voice: "This must be God's plan. He did not want the suffering to go on—my mother, my sister, and now Ben. No child of Ben will have to bear these demons anymore. Enough!" It was probably the bravest statement I have ever heard spoken aloud.

I hugged you. "You are so cold," I said, my eyes skating around the room. "You are a brave woman," I heard the policewoman say to me.

As your warrior soul searched for its final destination, I found a book by your bed, *Testo Junkie: Sex, Drugs, and Biopolitics in the Pharmacopornographic Era*. The book lays wide open, many of its pages marked with a yellow highlighter. It was written by Paul B. Preciado.[1]

What constitutes a real man or woman was something that had been on your mind for a while. We discussed it once, and you made it clear that the idea of a single "gender" did not apply to you. "I see the human, the person, and the sexual identity as a fluid progression and not as a binary division." As Preciado asserts; "I am not a woman and I am not a man."

This was my son talking—my own flesh and blood—yet I was unable to fully grasp his concepts and ideas; perhaps just a thin layer of it permeated.

Ten years before that day, I had received my master's degree in women's studies. There was not much emphasis or concern over the self as being fluid at that time. We were the defenders of women's rights: our bodies, the exclusion from elitism, workplace and the political sphere. Spoken and written language was identified as an instrument of patriarchal oppression toward women. I chose to research women's detective fiction, based on the assumption that the genre constitutes a platform for the expression of feminist theory. As part of my studies, I wrote about the woman detective as an androgynous model, building on Carolyn Heilbrun's philosophy. Heilbrun was an American academic and a prolific feminist author, who taught English literature at an Ivy League school while writing detective novels under the pen name Amanda Cross. She focused on the androgynous woman in an attempt to find an explanation for the two opposing stereotypical images of women in the literature: either as Eve or as Lilith. She spoke of an alternative model, one which grants the individual a wide range of social and psychological choices among those attributed to the two sexes. Heilbrun was a bit timid about her theory and did not extend it beyond the psychological and social arenas.

In Preciado's book, *Testo Junkie,* she recounts her own experience self-administering topical testost. She discusses the political aspects of drugs that transform the body, such as birth control, Viagra, Prozac, and estrogen: Technology allows us to better explore our body, whose geographical boundaries, in turn, become better capable of change at any time.

So true, I often thought to myself.

But, of course, none of these thoughts crossed my mind that Saturday evening. In fact, I did not think at all that night. It is only now, as I allow myself to revisit the day and the room, that I am able to suspend the moment, to take a break in repose and consider what was going through Ben's mind.

On your desk, which was jam-packed but in impeccable order, were placed: your white leather bracelet; one feather earring; and *Mode,* a record written and recorded by Goitia Deitz, your band: You are the Deitz and Jay is the Goita.[2] On it are five tracks of beautiful electronic music.

Placed in front of the record, I notice a photo book, *Omahyra and Boyd,* photographed by Ellen Von Unwerth. It is wide to a page that depicts two women or two men; it was not clear to me. And again, the question repeats itself: Who is the boy? Who is the girl?

"GIRLS WHO ARE BOYS WHO LIKE BOYS TO BE GIRLS WHO DO BOYS LIKE THEY'RE GIRLS WHO DO GIRLS LIKE THEY'RE BOYS..."[3]

This lyrical sentence, taken from the first page of the album's liner notes, sums it all up. No punctuation is involved, not even a system of symbols used to divide or clarify the text. It is a clear act of eliminating all emphasis on any part; let it be fluid. It should be sung as one long breath, on and on, at all times.

This is the last time that you and I will be in the same room. I continue to look around through my dusty, opaque glasses; my body feels amorphous and undefined. It is a noir movie that I am watching unspool from my own heart. *I must stay,* I keep ordering my body, an unknowable force whispering into my ear, "Don't you dare leave this room. You are not done."

On the left corner of your desk, I see a small postcard, a figure painted by your favorite artist, Egon Schiele.[4] In 2005, we went together to see the exhibit "Egon Schiele: The Ronald S. Lauder and Serge Sabarsky Collections at the Neue Galerie." Three full floors contained the expanse of Schiele's work. You went back twice more. The small postcard on your desk depicts a nude

figure of a woman, her thin, almost starved body is amorphous and obscured, yet erotic.

Once again, the question is asked: Was this person born with a vagina?[5] Is it a woman made to appear like a man, or both a man and a woman?

My grandfather, your great-grandfather, Isidor, watches over all of this from a photo above your desk, which you had carefully framed. He lived in Poprad, then part of the Austro-Hungarian empire, nowadays in Slovakia. He wears his Austro-Hungarian army uniform from the Great War. He looks young and handsome.

I was always told by my mother, with great pride, that he had served as an officer. This pride was not unusual as pointed out by Dr. Jacob Segall's book[6]: "[The] overwhelming majority of the Jewish population in the western half of the monarchy reacted with enthusiasm to the start of the war. They saw it as an opportunity to exhibit their patriotism and counter anti-Semitic prejudices. Behind this lay the desire to earn membership and respect by demonstrating Jewish commitment. During the First World War, over 300,000 Jewish soldiers served in the Austro-Hungarian army, 25,000 of them as reserve officers..."

The death stairs in Mauthausen concentration camp

More than 20 years later, at the age of 48, your great-grandpa would be taken by the same army he served to Mauthausen, a concentration camp in Austria. Their system was so ruthless and barbarous that Mauthausen was considered one of the worst concentration camps, even by concentration camp standards. Conditions were hard to bear, and the inmates suffered from malnutrition, abuse, and hard labor in the quarries. Temperatures dropped as low as -22°F, and prisoners were not entitled to any medication, not even first aid. All this led to a high mortality rate. Between August 8, 1938, and liberation on May 5, 1945, approximately 195,000 prisoners were held in Mauthausen. 150,000 of them are estimated to have perished.

Fred Friendly[7] wrote in May 19, 1945: "Mauthausen was built with a half-million rocks which 150,000 prisoners—18,000 was the capacity—carried up on their backs from a quarry 800 feet below. They carried it up steps so steep that a Captain and I walked it once and were winded, without a load. They carried granite and made 8 trips a day... and if they stumbled, the S.S. men pushed them into the quarry. There are 285 steps, covered with blood. They called it the steps of death."

As your soul is ascending, I can see that you have not forgotten to collect your great-grandfather's blood off the same steps that he was pushed down. You will be returning it to him, where it belongs; it is your offering for the bond between the two of you. This time, that bond will last forever.

Many years ago as a child, you wished that:

I had grown up poverty-stricken, a street boy and urban dweller of
the city. How can one test one's character and moral perseverance
when you don't go through any hardship? I don't need to push and
try to eke out a living, and I'm resentful because of it. No one is equal,
the caste system always exists, everyone wants to help but no one
wants to live like the people they're helping. Take everyone, rich, poor
and throw them down to that level, and you'll see who is truly strong.
One can't be trusted by the size of their hearts but by the hardships
they've lived through. if you see this, understand it. understand
living like shit. Try it once in a while. I don't know if I will, but I will
try. You just hear whatever and ever. Our religion is suffering. We
worship pain. Through suffering, one can be baptized into a wise and
emotional being. One is freed through suffering. I have not suffered.
I wish I had. Wish I had let myself fall into a glorious hole. But I have
not. It would be so good, to grow up bado. But I avoided the pain,
I was fucking pathetic weakling.

We are still in Ben's apartment. I pick up the phone to call my sister. My hands are shaking, and I cannot reach her; it is about 3 a.m. in Israel. I dial again, this time to a dear friend who I was able to reach at once, an ex-general in the police chief of the Israeli Fire Department; he is used to frantic calls in the middle of the night.

I yell, he tells me later, "Ben is dead! I can't reach my sister!" He takes matters into his own hands and within 24 hours, they will be coming to New York.

Not moving, I sit motionless on the black sofa, the one that Ben purchased from Ikea. We were there with him; we helped him to take it to his new apartment, where he assembled all the parts. He was very skilled at any activity that involved shaping fragments into compositions.

Our friends ████, ███████, ████, and my nephew, are all there. Together, we are in silence.

Ben is in his bed. We are waiting for the medical examiner to arrive. It takes some time; finally, he appears with a medical bag in his hand, and we wait in the other room. When he leaves, all that remains is to wait for the ambulance to pick Ben up for what would be his last journey. We ask our friends to go home; it is late and there is no reason for them to stay.

The two police officers are still there. They are gentle and polite.

When the ambulance arrives, I rush out of the apartment door, but Roger wants to stay. I stand on a dark street, alone, in that peripheral part of Brooklyn. I am unwilling to look toward the entrance of Ben's building. I don't want to see any more; I would rather go blind than stare at my son wrapped in a plastic bag, laying on a stretcher.

You are not here anymore. You locate yourself as kryptonite,[8] a manifestation of dust and torque:

> I wonder for those who can't, I hear a fingernail tapping on glass,
> I am manifest in kryptonite dust I pretended the wind isn't a razor
> I feel in the midst of revising the past from a safe vantage point,
> remembering seeing Bettie Page's initials in the lit end of a cigarette.
> Re living alcoholic japan in guitar Strings, so much naivete it makes
> me choke.
>
> —17 YEARS OLD

I am still here,
locating myself with my stolen child,
taken by the faery, nymph, and pixie;

"Come away, o human child!
To the waters and the wild
with a faery, hand in hand,
or the world's more full of weeping than you can understand." **9**

His Trouble & Bass partner Luca Venezia, better known to most as Drop The Lime, eulogized Ben in a message on Soundcloud attached to an early track of Luca's that Deitz produced:

> "In 2002, before Trouble & Bass even existed, I put together this compilation called "Nobody Compilate" of various young NYC-based artists, and Ben was the first to contribute and help curate the compilation. Given that we both went to the same high school, and shared strong punk rock roots, we illegally placed these home printed CD-R copies of the compilation in shops like HMV and Tower Records in sections like IDM, D&B, and Electronica to reach the right people and it hilariously caught buzz.

> "All that was printed for contact info was this random NBDYUNDRTHS_N@AOL.COM email address, but the excited/confused mails of — 'I tried to buy your CD and was told I could just have it for free as it wasn't in the system' were frequent. Soon after, Star Eyes joined forces as did Zack Shadetek, The Captain, and AC Slater, and the same DIY attitude evolved even more, creating Trouble & Bass into a label and crew. With the recent tragic passing of such a magical, influential, and driven soul, I wanted to share Ben's track with the world. It's such a strong and honest glimpse into the furiously original production of music he soon progressed into. You will be missed greatly Ben. We love you.

> "Trouble & Bass had just thrown its last ever party at Verboten nightclub in Brooklyn on April 18 with a lineup that included Drop The Lime, Jubilee, Addison Groove, Tony Quattro, Doctor Jeep and Petey Clicks. They released their final compilation at the end of March as well, which included music from Deitz."

Endnotes

1. Prior to transitioning, Preciado published some works under the name Beatriz Preciado. Paul B. Preciado has become one of the leading thinkers in the study of gender and sexuality. A professor of Political History of the Body, Gender Theory, and History of performance at Université Paris VIII, he is also the author of *Manifiesto contrasexual,* which has become a queer theory classic.

2. Cut Mistake Music, 2015.
Track list:
New Horizons 8:07
Sunday Shimmer 6:10
Falling Again 5:39
Temples 5:45
An Ocean 4:06

   Style: acid, house. Mixed by James Aparicio, Mastered by Taylor Deupree, Art and Design by Ciaran O' Shea. All of them were close friends of yours; now we have the great fortune of keeping in touch.

3. "Girls & Boys" by Blur

   "Streets like a jungle
   So call the police
   Following the herd
   Down to Greece
   On holiday
   Love in the 90s
   Is paranoid
   On sunny beaches
   Take your chances looking for

   [Chorus:]
   Girls who are boys
   Who like boys to be girls
   Who do boys like they're girls
   Who do girls like they're boys
   Always should be someone,
   you really love."

4. Scheile (1890–1918) was an Austrian painter. Schiele was a major figurative painter of the early 20th century. His work is noted for its intensity and its raw sexuality, and the many self-portraits. The twisted body shapes and the expressive line that characterize Schiele's paintings and drawings mark the artist as an early proponent of Expressionism.

5. discovermagazine.com/1992/jun/turningaman62 "Why Some Babies with Male Genes Have Female Parts." For further reading see *The Gene* by Siddhartha Mukherjee, p. 355–36.

6. "The German Jews as Soldiers in the War of 1914–1918, a Statistical Analysis." (1922).

7. www.jewishgen.org/databases/Holocaust/0117_Mauthausen-Gusen-Death-Book.html.

8. In science fiction, an alien mineral with the property of depriving Superman of his powers.

9. From "The Stolen Child" by William Butler Yeats.

The unseen — dreams

Indeed, your body is gone, but both your dreams and mine can stay alive. You kept a dream journal; it was well organized, on loose-leaf paper. At times you indicate dates, at times not. I have no clue why.

My own dreams bring back memories of familiar physical sensations between the two of us, from times when words were not spoken. Instead, silent contemplation and insight prevailed. I read your journal, am glimpsing into your mind I am not dreaming. You are here.

Art by Chagit Deitz

BEN'S DREAMS:

Undated

We're driving through the drape of fog and driving to the sea and the headlights are a projector and the road is a movie screen and the moon is a blasted white thing and we pass fields filled with a million bent blades of grass and he's sitting next to me while I'm driving and he's staring at the blasted white thing of the moon and we're listening to the radio and I see his jaw twitch in the blue light as the smoke of his cigarette gets sucked out of the window and we're silent and all I want is to reach out and touch his cheek, touch the twitch of his jaw, touch the fuzz of the har at the base of his neck. I see the milky reflection of the eyes of a deer off in a field through the smoke and fog watching us as we pass.

We get to the beach I run he follows we race on the sand he grabs me we fall we roll and the moon is a white thing in the sky that lays its light on the Atlantic and upon our tumbling bodies lying in the sand breathing hard, we hold each other for a second frozen. The grass sways.

I stand to take off my clothes and run towards the water and I look back at him and just as I'm about to go under I see him move his clothes off and running and when I emerge he's there beside me our bodies smooth and salty and glistening like real alive breathing things, blasted under the moon and blasted into memory like smoke blown from anxious, tender lips.

10/21/12

Two men are in a printing press. It is the 1930s. They are prototypical gangsters. They are practicing to beat each other up for some reason. The printing press starts running and their fake fight turns into a real one, with one of the men getting crushed inside a roller. Outside, "Beer 1990," the girlfriend of one of the men, waits for her boyfriend to come out with another young woman she has just met. They find themselves in the apple house, an apple pie diner that appears to have been closed for years. Despite this several men are in the kitchen. Beer's friend inquiries as to where the apple pie is. The men are angry and refuse to help. Now Beer 1990 and her woman friend are a young squat foul-mouthed boy and his borderline retarded adult friend. The boy says that without him his adult friend "couldn't keep his pecker hard," implying that he has mental control over him. One of the men in the kitchen of the restaurant becomes furious and shows the

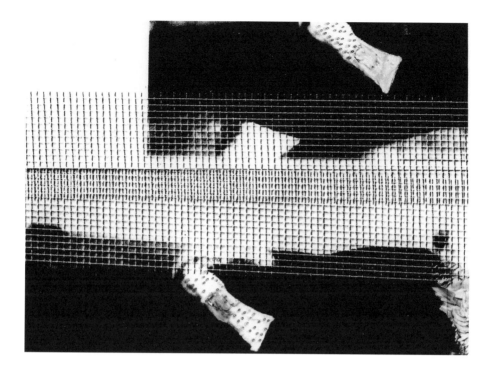

boy and his friend sketched drawings. The drawings imply some sort of program wherein female turtles are implanted with some sort of embryo so as to give birth to some sort of hybrid creature. The drawings portray various strange alien and crustacean-esque creatures crawling from beneath the sand on a beach, slowly rising from their birth and lumbering to shore. Evil things are imminent.

11/03/12

A young man travels around the world trying to meet those who have skills of which there is no historical precedent. He meets a pipe bender (a man who can bend metal pipes into whatever shape he wishes) in Scotland, a framer (not a typo) named Dubs in Ireland, and a dying holy man in India.

11/05/12

I am with my father. He goes to a fancy dinner while I go to a fast food seafood restaurant that is within some sort of cheap resort. I order the "Reggae Party," a seafood platter. There is a parade of giant die-cast toys that my father reminisces about seeing when he was younger. He talks about how he would watch and photograph it for hours, and how it stretched off into the distance.

Art by Chagit Deitz

11/15/12

It is the future. People are getting full body plastic surgery, their bodies covered in sutures and stitches. They lay in nutrient baths and gossip. They talk about the need for freedom and for space in the overcrowded colony worlds. Their answer is to start wars on other planets to wipe out the colonies there, thus allowing the wealthy to travel to these planets and have beautiful views and vistas. They travel to these other planets in ships that then convert into walking multi-legged housing units. Unbeknownst to them though, their enemy has stowed away as running machines that are secretly programmed to cause chaos and destroy the whole colonization operation.

3/29/13

I am a member of a rich waspy family vacationing on an island (maybe Fire Island) or by the beach. I am having an affair with ███████████, who is bound to be taken away by our parents and used in some sort of military project because of the powers she has. Later there is a sort of gathering where a famous ambulance driver who looks like Bon Jovi is asked to sing. Sadly someone has cut the chords to his mic and replaced them with their own so that it appears that he cannot sing. I drive with him in the ambulance and he speeds along careening through the streets. I tell him how exciting it is. Later my son is delivered to me from the hospital wrapped in a carapace of cloth. I must rip away the cloth to reveal the child within.

12/10/13

I am running through the dirty streets of a city, naked, running through the encompassing darkness. A woman friend is turned on by this. At another point, I look at my reflection in the mirror and I have no eyeballs, just reddish white colored eyes with no pupils.

I have a dream:

June 2017

I display all of my good valuable jewelry in a "jewelry show." Other vendors are stationed around me. It is time to pack up and go. I don't see my jewels anymore; someone else has packed them with their goods. I know who it is and want it back, but no such luck, so I decided to steal some jewelry and precious ornaments. Roger thinks it is a good idea, and as I finish my task the goods are placed in a baby carriage, where baby Ben is sleeping. His resting body covers the stolen goods, and, without fear, we march out.

In real life, most of my jewelry is kept in a safe; it is too fancy or expensive to wear. It is mine because other people have died, mostly relatives who ceased to live under tragic circumstances: Roger's mother who died at 43; his younger sister, my great aunt, the one who my mother adored, murdered in Auschwitz. Now all of them are a pile of personal adornments from the past.

Ben is the last one to pass on, my most precious jewel. Now he is "gathered unto his people," as the bible verse says *(Genesis 15:5)*. It is etched into my mind and thoughts, a verse rich in significance.

"ואתה תבוא אל-אבותיך בשלום תקבר בשיבה טובה:
דור רביעי ישובו הנה כי לא-שלם עון האמרי עדי-הנה"

"You shall go to your fathers in peace; you shall be buried at a good old age. But in the fourth generation, they shall return here, for the iniquity of the Amorites is not yet complete."

"Thou shalt go to thy fathers in peace." Abram's ancestors had died in Babylonia, but the phrase, used here for the first time, invokes the concept of the immortality of the soul. The body may be buried far away, but the soul joins the company of its forefathers in some separate abode, not to be absorbed, but still to enjoy a personal existence."[10]

Endnote

10. From *A Bible Commentary for English Readers* by Charles Ellicott, 1877.

20 years ago

Twenty years ago, Roger and I are spending the weekend in Casco, Maine. Ben stayed home. Roger had to leave a day early due to a work obligation, I remain in the house alone. It is Sunday, July 12, and Ben is calling me. "Mom, Dr. ███████████ from ███████████ Hospital in Kansas just called me saying that Peggy (Roger's sister) is in the hospital in critical condition. She swallowed everything in her medicine cabinet…here is his phone number, please call him." The physician who called so frantically did not even bother to check who this young voice was on the other side of the line, answering his phone call.

Ben, not even 19 years old, received the distraught call. By this time, responsibility is already burdening his slender young shoulders. Ben acted quickly, did not waver, and made all the necessary calls, to me, to a crucial friend of Peggy's. He handled it.

Peggy died on July 16, Roger's birthday. We all gathered in Kansas where she had lived, to participate in a surreal dream-like church service. Peggy had converted to Catholicism and belonged to two churches. Hundreds of people who we had never met came to say their last goodbye and cried in our arms.

Roger could not even walk. Ben was the one who held strong and assisted him to the gravesite.

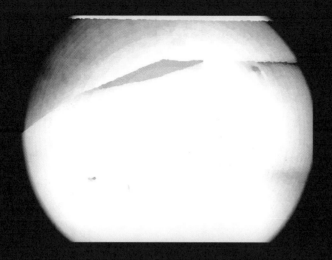

this is the darkest place
cold and clay skin against gray walls
I watched my father throw
himself upon your casket
I read your poems but
i could not
look your dead face in the eye
i wept
i actually wept
but
i have never been so afraid
as i was of you
and silence through it all
through shudders gasp and subtle
they lay like freshly pressed sheets
wrapped tight around your face
the stillborn drone of the highway
as it penetrates the shade of my room
at night
and is conjoined with a cold clay moonlight
fractured and cast upon my bed
a moon that a million eyes are upon
eyes that count thoughtlessly
        into dreaming
                        but i am still awake
and i am still thinking

It is now October 27, 2017, seven days before what would have been your 35th birthday. A dream visits me at night:

> A man is holding an adorable baby boy. The baby sees me, smiles, and stretches his hands toward me. He wants me to hold him. I take him into my arms. He turns around, looking toward the man who had been holding him before; he wants to go back, unto him.

I cannot avoid seeing the number 7 as a dominant one in this dream. The date, year, and number of days before your birthday. I think: seven days of the week, seven colors of the rainbow, the seven deadly sins, seven days of Chatan Kallah[11] and seven days of Shiva.[12]

Endnotes

11. *Chatan Kallah:* bride and groom.

12. *shiv'ah:* seven days of mourning after the death of a family member.

Art by Chagit Deitz

Polka-dotted blanket from Bloomingdale's

Near the end of my pregnancy in late October of 1982, I passed by Bloomingdale's on 63rd Street and could not resist going in. The polka-dotted baby blanket was calling my name; I made a quick purchase, going against all of my prejudices and beliefs.

As I brought it home, I could not foresee how this object would become so precious to you, my son. Growing up you used to drag it around everywhere, all of the time. It's in bad shape already, but that doesn't matter to you; you keep holding it tightly, with a force that hints at your character and the temperament that will define your way later in life.

██████, the woman who babysat for you and a few other kids at her home, was pretty upset with you clinging onto this blanket. I knew that I had to be polite with her—she was a rigid but excellent sitter. I begged for more time for you to let go. She agreed.

Pleasant to the touch and smell, and close to your body, you took comfort in this soft, fuzzy, almost reduced to a pulp, blanket. A new magical realization was dawning on you: "Mother is not me," but she is here with me. It was a realization for me as well: "You are not me, but you are here."

Ben was growing up, searching for an escape route, and I would have to learn to watch him carefully from a distance. This was the beginning of a long and frightening journey toward independence for both of us. A journey that did not guarantee success at all times. We were constantly walking on this thin rope; at times we fell.

This magical blanket had all the hallmarks of a traditional handmade baby quilt, one that welcomes a new baby into the family and community. The textile was composed of three layers: the top layer, which is usually the decorated part; the middle, a layer of batting or other similarly soft material; and a

back, made out of plain cloth—all attached together by the quilting technique. It has been customary for centuries for women who share a strong bond to come together as a group to express their artistic gifts and share a social space. Eager to participate in these private events, they would bring scraps of old fabric from home, pieces of tattered garments, torn blankets, or any other useless cloth. As new fabric was too expensive for many to purchase at the turn of the last century, many were determined to bestow used material with new life, in the form of a baby quilt. Such quilts form women's visual narratives of countless past stories and events that are now transmitted to future generations by textile, thin thread and stitching.

I imagine that when so many hands are at work, a prickly needle might hurt a laboring finger and a drop of blood would then stain the cloth. Perhaps countless women's hands try to wipe the spot off, but the bleeding history of a woman—maybe a mother, a sister, a grandmother, or a friend—continues to hide under the surface, bleeding her history. Perhaps this is how your blanket came to be.

Aside from welcoming you into the world, baby Ben, the dotted blanket gave you the freedom you needed to reach out and explore new territories, to dive in full force into unearthly universes, spaces where you could weave illusions of mystical reality. At the same time, the blanket also served as much needed aid for the difficult negotiation between your inner and outer realities: the worlds of fantasy and real life. Like any successful outcome of a negotiation or mediation, both sides must be validated. Your creative energy must be allowed to spring forth while you remain protected from any worries.

You are the ruler of the universe, the most skillful king without ever losing your queen mother. Later on, it will become clear that this space of transition will serve you well: Your creative force will come to dominate your life.

In my mind, I am watching you play with your little figurines; speaking to and with them, assembling wooden blocks into various structures; driving cars at any speed you desire, at times until they crash into buildings or other objects. Other times you order them to slow down," behave," and act gently. Still, you remain the boss.

You write:

My life has been intertwined with escapism, and more often than not, my chosen escape has been into the realms of science fiction. If I had to guess, my earliest initiation into the realms of sci-fi were with the original Star Wars trilogy ("Return of the Jedi" came out the year after I was born), watched and re-watched ad infinitum on hazy VHS tapes in my attic. I was a young reader, as well, and can remember days spent at home suffering from an asthma attack, strapped to my ventilator machine, reading Isaac Asimov or Orson Scott Card. I remember having a large paperback collection of Asimov's robot stories with lovely black and white illustrations in it that I spent years devouring. Asimov enthralled me with his generations spanning sagas that included his Robot, Galactic Empire and Foundation series. At 10 or 11, however, a moment as pivotal as my first viewing of Star Wars occurred when I watched "Akira" for the first time. I was not only introduced to anime but to science fiction as well, and a lifelong love affair was born. Both "Akira" and "Blade Runner," which I would view several years later, would crystallize in my mind [as] my ideal science fiction aesthetic.

At the age of 20, I read "Valis" and was dragged into the paranoiac worlds of Philip K. Dick, who remains my favorite science fiction author to this day. I went on a reading spree, digesting every book of his that I could get my hands on. "A Scanner Darkly" remains his most personally resonant tale, one that brings me to tears time and again. As time has progressed, my tastes in science fiction have become more obscure. I recently discovered Wim Wenders' brilliant "Until The End of the World," and loved it so much that a friend and I watched the 5-hour director's cut of the film I have become friends with Stuart Argabright, a musician whose band Black Rain did the score for the "Necromancer" audiobook, as well as for the film "Johnny Mnemonic." I've discovered the work of Sogo Ishii and his film "Burst City." Finally, in the last few years, I've discovered perhaps my greatest "Blade Runner," I collect retro-tech such as LCD glasses and portable CD players, and even have a pair of hangable Flogiston chairs, like the ones featured in the movie "The Lawnmower Man." Science fiction to me has become more than an escape [to me]. It's a way of life."

Does your fear of autonomy lead you to a fantasy world? Is it possible that imitating fantasy caused you to live on the edge, as well as taking many risks? Indeed, to the outside observer, you were brave, but at the same time, your heart was trembling.

"The mystical life is the center of all that I do and all that I think and all that I write." [13]

"As a young girl, she would chase butterflies and stomp ants' nests, hidden from parental view and ensconced in an imaginary world too large to be contained in dreams. As she stomped ants nests, she was a giantess, huge and all-knowing and surveying the tiny world beneath her."

The text quoted above is taken from one of Ben's stories. It is one of the many "fables" he wrote: narratives that tell of the forces of nature, magic, animals, and plants, always providing a moral lesson.

Most of his stories do not have a title or a specific location, and at times the date is missing; I imagine that the following story takes place in Maine. Perhaps it is only my own fantasy, as his reality is unknown, but as a young child, he used to spend summers in our summer home, a place loved by us all. As Roger would fly into the City every Monday for work and return on Thursday nights, our weekdays were a "Mommy and Me" mini summer camp. Every morning Ben would swim to his hidden place, a small rocky island surrounded by pine trees and water and lily pads. At times he managed to "transport" some miniature action figures along with him, devising plots of bravery.

At night, lying down in that absolute darkness, Ben would continue to devise a plan for the following day, then wake up in the morning filled with excitement and ready to set the new game into motion. Those were the happiest times of his life; he had a free space for dreams and for the imagination to flow, with no fear of an audience. He was at his best, making connections between his own heart and mind.

When summer was almost gone, at the beginning of September, it was time to go back to NY to our permanent home, and for Ben to start a new year in school. We would pack our belongings and drive south away from Maine. Arriving home, usually at night or in the early evening, it would be quiet around us, maybe a car or two passing by or a dog barking in the distance.

One year, a Crimson Gallicas rose by our front fence was still blooming, and the loudest noise came from crickets chirping nearby, moving their wings as they communicated with each other. I recall your curiosity, "Why are they so loud here? And not in Maine?"

Indeed, my son, you are right, but I don't have an answer.

It was the sound of the ghosts that kept her awake at night. In the blackest hours, the wails of distant apparitions would come whistling into her bedroom, palpitant and benumbed and echoing through the pine and oak. They birthed unquiet visions that unfurled as she lay enveloped in the prickling wool of her blanket: bats erupting out of the dark like inky founts from some atramentous spring, bridges stretched broken and crooked across unknowable abysses, bestial and tameless things alive and alight in embers of boreal flame and all manner of inchoate terrors made manifest at the precipice of all envisioning.

In time she would come to recognize these emanations as the transient passage of automobiles along the serpentine bends of the nearby interstate. Yet in the otherworldly place that lay between sleep and waking these cries served as maleficent enticements to movement like ancient played in baleful and disconsolate tones upon the foliar instrumentation of the forest, tones which shook the brittle autumn leaves from their arboreal perches and sent them clattering against her window in arrhythmic punctuation to the eidolic sibilates of the night.

As she lay she felt as if a thin taut cord had been tied around her belly, a wispy tendril of a thing that unwound from her bed and through her door and down the stairs and out onto the road that would one day bear her father's name, pulling and begging at her until she could lay still no more.

She lifted the blanket and slipped silently from the warmth of the bed, her feet slapping coldly against the chilled wood as she hopped out. She picked her coat up off its hanger and slipped her feet into her moccasins and padded out of her room with an economy of movement that cast vaguely feline shadows along her traverse.

As she passed through the hallway her thin legs moved with the assiduously measured rhythm of a clock, each rise, and fall accompanied by the abrading exhalations of her sleeping father's breath and the noisy compression of the ancient floorboards like the soft perpetuate crush of snow on frozen ponds. She made her way down the stairs and to where the torch hung from a nail at the front door. She unhooked it and opened the door, pushing back the rustling covey of mosquitoes that chattered in sibilant conversation about the door light like anxious parents.

She stepped down the front steps and onto the road, its pebbled dissolution draped in the grey cast of the moon like an ashen epimandylion, and the whole of the land frozen and adumbral in the inspissate light as if some silvered cloth had been smoothed against the asperous surface of the earth. She followed the winding cilia of the road past Watkins' farm, the cows in the field asleep and frozen in the milky illumination like beneficent idols amongst the softly swaying saw blades of bromegrass. Further along, she passed the old barn which stood like some wooden dolmen, its sides covered in a slowly encroaching lamina of ivy and the dead and dying grass unfurling at its base in a dissolution yellow nimbus. Its broken windows were like eyes voided of care and its single flickering lantern illuminated a halo of insects like ink splotches set starkly against yellow parchment. Its ancient and crumbling wood was cinereal in color and had weathered storms now spoken of in hushed and pusillanimous tones. She crossed over the road and towards the rear of the barn where a solitary elm stood atop a small hill that looked down upon a shallow valley of cedar, the wispy curls of its branches outstretched in a grand and alluvial testament to the domed nothingness above. A tatterdemalion swing hung limply beneath the unfurling canopy of jagged leaves, shaking slightly in the breeze.

She climbed the hill and passed under the blackened shade of the tree as above her the writhing branches carved great grey puzzle pieces into the blank heavens. She continued along through the field, following the road's path as it descended towards the forest, the sky above her like an upturned cauldron whose spilled contents flowered discordantly upon the once barren landscape below. The grass threshed softly underfoot as she descended the hill, the whole of the field atremble with the stuttering hiss of the crickets and the stars above like Luminant dandelions in the sky.[14] Her wandering thoughts kept the insipid fear of the night away. She picked her way through where gnarled roots which burst from the earth, twisting the path. As she proceeded the forest began to encroach carelessly on the path, the cedar trees indifferent to the sad trespassed of man. She passed the McGovern's house, a small A-frame nestled within the embrace of small bushes and ferns. She approached the woodpile, covered in blue tarpaulin that pooled rainwater. Her torch illuminated a conical spotlight ahead of her, the rest of the blind forest a heaving, alive that that exhaled with the breath of a thousand chirping crickets, buzzing mosquitoes and squirrels which crashed electrically through the brittle leaves left dead and unmoving on the forest floor (the tiny muscles of a squirrel, the wings of a mosquito, the eyes of a moth). She could still hear the ghosts, as well as the plaintive cry of a loon (the sound of the ghosts was now joined by the plaintive cry of the loon) the two mournful echoes merging into a sad cacophony which reverberated amidst the wilderness. As she passed the McGovern's their dog began to bark, a friendly quick yelp of recognition. She approached the post to which he was tied, cupping her hands about its head and nuzzling gently against his face, nose to nose. There was a fearful beauty alive in the forest which reflected in the bubbling spring which ran through a small roadside ditch. Lily pads dotted the surface like floating pavilions that housed spiders and water bugs that dances across the pockmarked surface of the water like pellets of rain. She switched on her torch as she entered the water. The loon resumed its mournful cry, a cry of such terse resonance that she imagined it echoing off the very moon itself, reflected back onto some far off quiet place where it drenched the silence like a malediction or a please her bare feet were sticky now, clots of pine tar gumming up the soles of her feet. And still the ghosts cried, and still the loon called out, both voices of sadness in the forested dark, rising and falling like waves, shaking the trees with the sheer force of their sadness. She pressed on. She had taken this path a thousand times as. As a young girl, she would chase butterflies and stomp ants nests, hidden from parental view and ensconced in an imaginary world too large to be contained in dreams. As she stomped ants nests she was a giantess, huge and all knowing and surveying the tiny world beneath her. The sky had been left drained in messy puddles strewn about the path, and she took

her moccasins off, wading through the cool water. then stopped, her actions having stirred within herself a memory.

She saw in her mind's envisioning her father's calming face as he sat at her bedside, his features illuminated by trembling candlelight. She felt the blanket tucked tightly around her bony shoulders, saw the snowflakes falling outside her window like coral orbs through the ebony abyss of the night and saw her father's eyes, fulgid in the quavering illumination, as he spoke softly to her.

A long time ago the animals had a gathering, he said. The lions and the elephants bears and zebras, the moose and the deer and all the animals the bears too complained of having their fish eaten by men. The deer said that the humans were eating too many of their berries. Every animal had their say, and everyone voiced a complaint. They were all in agreement that something had to be done. They talked all day and all night until the last dying embers of their fire set their stern faces alight in the darkness, and all were huddled about the fire in quiet judgment. They had reached a decision. They would eat the humans. The Lions were particularly excited, and the bears as well, and all were ready to go about their solemn and sad work. But there was one dissenting voice amongst the crowd. High pitched and timid, it was the smallest creature of all, the mosquito, who cleared his throat and addressed the crowd. If you would be so kind, said the mosquito. All of you have voiced your complaints about the humans, but none of you have said one kind thing. I would like to speak on their behalf. For if it was not for man, we mosquitoes would cease to be. You see while the humans are eating all your food, they themselves provide us with our meals. How could you be so cruel as to send the mosquitoes to their demise? The animals became hushed, the sad realization of the consequence of their decision now sinking in. Forgive us gentle mosquito. We shall let the humans live, for we cannot so cruelly condemn your kind to extinction. The mosquito thanked the lion, and all the animals returned to their respective lands, all in agreement to let us walk the earth freely, never knowing how close we came to our end.

She was left calmed by this demulcent remembrance and continued forth through the night with quiet, assured steps. ❖

One day upon arriving back home from Fire island I realized that the blue bag that contained your blanket had been forgotten on the island or on the ferry. Fear, concern, and anxiety envelop me. "What is the right move?" I ask myself. Being an incredibly smart little guy, there was no escape from sharing the news with you. My fear was real, and even though you did not cry out loud, the expression on your face and the absence of any sound said it all.

In a similar vein, I remember times when we traveled to Fire Island on cold days to "help" dad with his chores. Roger bought that house many years ago before we got married and Ben was born. Eventually, the place became a summer rental property as we preferred lakes, pine trees, and open spaces, and spent our summers in Maine. We would visit the Island before and after the rental season (from late May to early September) as off-season guests. Roger would busy himself with the much-needed tasks of repairing, securing, restoring, fixing and cleaning the house. Ben and I were left with almost nothing to occupy ourselves with.

You were quick to find solutions. At the age of 3 or 4 you pulled the First Aid book from the damp bluish bookshelf and started "reading" it. It later turned out that you *really had* read and understood it all, as we learned when we received long explanations about the ailments and dangerous species on the island. Of course, you knew all about the correct treatment of each symptom. I was assured of being safe from any harm.

Our house on the island was not at all immune from Sandy, the big storm that hit the Northeast in 2012. It was completely destroyed.

In 2016, when Roger sold the now-empty lot, I did not join him for the closing. Coming home, he broke the silence; "I actually cried," he said. "It was the first house that I bought, the house where we had our wedding party, the place where allergic baby Ben would get stung by the nasty flies..."

Immediately upon realizing the blanket was missing, I shared it with Ben and, as mentioned above, he was quietly sad. However, from that day on, Ben exchanged the blanket with my nose: A new habit of stroking my nose was born. Usually after a few hours of not seeing me, or just sitting on my lap, he would reach up. I believe it was his way of showing how close he felt to me. This habit continued until Ben was 7 or 8 years old.

I still remember how at the end of the school day I would wait for you by the classroom door. "Here you are, I can see you." You would erupt out of the classroom toward me calling: "IMA!" followed by a big hug and a gentle touch of my nose. I am smiling even now.

When we visited you on Thursday night, May 7, the last night of your life, you gave me the same big hug (this time not touching my nose), and it was a solid embrace. It will forever signify the bond between our two hearts, two hearts that will continue to expand throughout life.

Endnotes

13. By William Butler Yeats (1865–1939) taken from Jamie James' "W.B. Yeats, Magus" in *Lapham's Quarterly*.

14. Luminant is a Texas-based electric utility.

Flâneur[15]

"There was the pedestrian who wedged into the crowd, but there was also the flâneur who demanded elbow room and was unwilling to forego the life of the gentleman of leisure… Around 1840 it was briefly fashionable to take turtles for a walk in the arcades. The flâneurs liked to have the turtles set the pace for them."

— WALTER BENJAMIN

"Maybe I've spent a lifetime trying to escape to places, I'd be forced to escape from."

— BEN

When I was a young girl growing up, my parents liked to stroll around Tel Aviv. Almost every Saturday night, they would experience and absorb the city and its surroundings. Flâneuring, or *shpazirin*, as they called it in the German language, so well-spoken by them and between them. The Hebrew language does not offer a comparable phrase that evokes the same sensation and emotions. They loved to walk in Tel Aviv, a familiar territory, not in order to "get" something or to visit friends, but instead simply to wander around, check how other people dressed and talked, to examine new products in storefronts, to connect to the outside world. An anonymous couple among others, constructing a new narrative for their banal lives. There were times when I liked to join them, strolling along the streets, hovering among fresh and unfamiliar milieu, discovering and rediscovering the magical panorama.

Virginia Woolf, in *Street Haunting: A London Adventure* (1930), portrays a similar experience: "*Passing, glimpsing, everything seems accidentally but miraculously sprinkled with beauty…*" She recollects that the "shores" of Oxford Street had nothing but treasure. "No thoughts of purchasing anything, it is just the eye flirting with the imagination of buying the beautiful ornaments, furniture that will fill the house that does not exist, 'the rug will do for the hall.

Art by Paul Gavani, 1842

That alabaster bowl will stand on the carved table...' but there is no obligation to own it... Let us choose those pearls, for example, and then imagine how, if we put them on, life would be changed." And with that, she concludes the adventure.

As time progressed, the tradition of *shpazritin* was "inherited" by Ben. As a young boy still dependent on my company, his interests and hobbies led us down many unknown roads. We walked the streets of Chinatown in NYC looking for robots, Chinese comics, and art books; we visited forgotten shopping centers in Maine that had old records (the start of his vast collection) and comic books. Casablanca Comics was another magical place; they not only sold old and new comics, they allowed Ben to trade some of his unwanted comics for more desirable ones—a fantastic deal for a true col-

lector. Carefully, he would wrap them in plastic envelopes.

When traveling to Tel Aviv with us, Ben would bring boxes full of old unwanted comic books to sell to the owner of a tiny comic book store on 152 Dizengoff Street. I have lived in Tel Aviv most of my life but had never come across it. Ben was probably the first Jewish comic book trader; luckily, *X-Men, Superman, The Justice League,* and others did not require a visa when entering Israel, as they were considered to be "Jewish heroes" by

the immigration officer. Coming back to the US, they enjoyed the same privilege, as Americans prefer their superheroes to come back home. We provided the airfare.

I was visiting Tel Aviv in February of 2018. After taking a yoga class, having dinner by myself and drinking too much vodka, not wanting to drive, I decided to take a quick stroll to the nearby Dizengoff Street. The past and present were mixing in my mind, taunting me. The landscape was that of my childhood, my restless teens, and Ben and Roger 25 years ago, and yet, I thought, "I am here now." And then all of a sudden I passed by that same comic

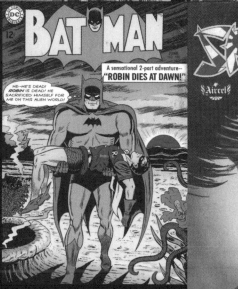

and second-hand bookstore. There was no change in its appearance; here, time stood still, and I experienced the spell of a mysterious space, never-ending to its fullest. Profoundly here: past, present, and future everywhere within me.

"All the devices we've invented so far are working away to tell us what time it is, but no one really knows what we are actually measuring. We are just using mechanical movements to track the passage of time because that is an approach our brains can latch onto. But the nature of time itself is still illusory." [16]

Radio Shack in Windham, Maine, had a "secret collection" of old records tucked away in the back of the store. Like you had done before with comic books, you were successful in convincing the manager of the place to give you access to these shabby boxes and take (for a small fee) whatever your heart desired. You obviously wanted most of them. Later, as music became the most important chapter of your life, these records would serve you well, for your own mixes and musical inspiration.

From your journal:

"My name is Ben, I am also an artist, an empathic and intelligent person, and not too bad on the eyes either. I am thirty-one years alive. I have lived a life filled with both wonder and horror, a life in which I have experienced the depth of both the external and internal worlds. I have traveled around the globe and witnessed many beautiful sights: seen a thousand fireflies casting their resplendent effulgence upon a valley in the Japanese countryside, watched dandelion clocks alight on the air like scintillate anemones in the Louisiana Bayou, and gazed upward at the sky cut into great blue puzzle pieces by tree branches in the forest of Maine. I have performed music to delirious crowds of heaving bodies in Paris, Berlin, Sydney, Montreal, and everywhere in between. I've been featured in many magazines all across the world, from *Dazed & Confused* to *NME*. I've released numerous records in a wide variety of musical styles, all of which have been highly regarded; international dance hits, post-punk inspired Goth, contemplative folktronica and krautrock and kosmische inspired synthesizer experimentations."

Ben performed music in so many cities around the world that it would be almost crass to list them all—at least 33 cities from Berlin to Sydney and back.

He got into trouble once upon arriving in Scotland, when he was asked by the immigration officer to present a work permit that was required even for one-time performances. As it turned out, his manager did not supply him with one, and even though the officer treated Ben very kindly, he was not allowed to enter the country. Upset, nervous, and tired, he flew to Berlin for one night on his way home to Brooklyn. It was a traumatic and agonizing experience for him. As always, he could not just "let it go," but replayed the events over and over in his mind.

Later, every time he would fly back to Great Britain to visit friends, he would be held up by the immigration officers for a long inquiry session into the purpose of his visit. We were there with him once, witnessing this unpleasant experience. Even though he was upset, it was clear to us that he showed integrity and wisdom in understanding the situation. mm, they promised Ben that his name would be removed from some list, so that in the future he would be allowed into the county no questions asked.

Ben and Roger were supposed to fly together to London at the end of May, 2015. Ben was still nervous, but Roger assured him that everything was going to be alright.

Ben passed on May 8.

His troubles with British immigration were over. Our anguish and painful reflection upon existence, however, had just begun.

After your passing, Adesh Deosaran wrote
on Facebook that on Thursday, July 1st, 2004
"…*we had what became the final Record Camp party at
the Knitting Factory in Tribeca. We booked a kid that no
one had ever heard of to play his first show. He showed
up with a desktop computer, am ugly beige PC complete
with a giant monitor and clunky keyboard. After about
an hour of technical difficulties, he was finally ready to
open the show. He played like a pro and blew us away.
It was pretty clear that this was his first and last
opening slot. He was a mysterious genius with
a young face and gray hair…*"

Indeed, only 2 years later, in 2006, you wrote that things *"began to fall into place for me musically."* You were mapping out your long and winding musical path, the one that would accompany you for the rest of your life: a flow of continuous musical creation, never stopping at any one name or style.

We, your parents, were somewhat removed from your musical world; you liked to keep it private, something that belonged only to you. We were totally unfamiliar with electronic music. It is hard to connect to music that belongs to a different world, culture, and personal memories. We all have a so-called "musical memory," which pushes us to connect with familiar tunes. Electronic music was miles away from either of our musical memories. Me, with Israeli songs sung in Hebrew and the melancholy Greek music rumbling out of the taverns. And Roger, as Ben used to tease him, lived in a time capsule: for him, American tunes from the 30s and 40s prevailed.

From Ben's journal:

"In 2006, things began to fall into place for me musically. I released my first EP, *The Most Lethal Dance,* under the alias Math Head. I was invited to Paris to play my first international show (which was

broken up by the riot squad mere minutes before I was about to go on stage). During the summer, I did a month-long European tour, playing in Rotterdam, Den Haag, Ghent, Vienna, Hamburg, Berlin, and elsewhere. This was my first taste of crippling anxiety, however, as I suffered for weeks before the tour, and was terrified for no good reason. I would become painfully familiar with this feeling.

I returned from the tour revitalized by an interest in the burgeoning dubstep and new rave scenes and eager to move in a new direction musically. I created a new alias, Passions, with which I intended to make music that I could play to anyone on the street and make them dance. I soon released the Dirty Deeds EP, which was my take on dubstep, which had just begun to catch people's ears at the time. I was incredibly excited about dubstep, especially because I was getting in on the ground floor of a musical movement. Instead of being a follower, I was a progenitor and originator, one of a handful of Americans producing and DJing this music. Nevertheless, this was a musical genre that had its roots in the UK, and there were not [yet] many outlets for it in the US.

Photo of a review from *NME* magazine

Thusly I, myself, and my then-friend Luca (Drop the Lime) decided to start a monthly party in which we could play the kind of music that we wanted to hear in New York. This would be an outlet not only for dubstep but for the emergent new French house scene as well as classic rave records that we grew up on. We formed a DJ crew along with our friends Vivian (Star Eyes) and Zack (Shadetek) called Trouble & Bass.

The first Trouble & Bass party was an instant success. Suddenly I was part of the hottest new thing in nightlife. I had gone from DJing solely in my bedroom to playing one of the most popular parties in Williamsburg at the time. I was overwhelmed. My anxiety was uncontrollable at that point, and I would be deathly afraid before every party we threw. After I was done DJing my set, I would torture myself internally, thinking that I had done a terrible job. As someone who likes to deal with people one on one, I felt completely overwhelmed by the need to be attendant to a hundred people at every party, to make each one feel like I was paying attention and that I cared. What's worse is that I thought there was something wrong with me for feeling this way. I felt like I was supposed to be having the time of my life, and that I must be broken in some way for not being able to shut off my internal monologue and just have fun.

Around this time I produced a song as Passions entitled "Emergency." "Emergency" spread through the internet via popular music blogs, and within a matter of weeks, my name was on everyone's lips. Artists and magazines and blogs that I had looked up to and adored were now telling me how brilliant I was.[17]

MSTRKRFT was perhaps the biggest American production outfit to emerge during the dance music renaissance. They were incredibly popular and influential, having been born out of the ashes of equality popular band DFA 1979. When I went to see them on my birthday in 2006 I told them how honored I was to meet them, and they responded by saying how honored they to meet me, and asked me how I made "Emergency," as they thought the track was brilliant.

I was soon being courted by a major dance music record label who wanted to press up 10,000 copies of "Emergency" and give me a major booking agent. Yet I had no idea what to do and what was the right decision. I had never been in a situation like this before, having instantaneous popularity with no one in my corner to help guide me. I tried to take things slowly and use my intuition but I truly did not know what the right path was. It was all happening so fast. In the end, I decided to sign to Kitsuné, an uber-cool French label that was the hippest thing going at the moment.[18]

It was a huge mistake in terms of my career, as they put absolutely no promotion behind the record whatsoever, did not help me get an agent or manager, and did not pay me until I hired a French lawyer to hassle them. The original label that wanted to sign me would have guaranteed me a high-paying successful career as a DJ, but, considering how things ended up playing out, perhaps it's best that I didn't sign with them. Either way, I have no regrets over my decision, if anything I feel sorry for the confused and overwhelmed 24-year-old who was thrown into the deep end of the pool without even a lifeguard on duty.

In 2007, Passions' explosive electro-punk debut single "Emergency" swept the dance charts, gaining instant acclaim. Ben had high hopes for live gigs, willing his audiences to *"fight without hitting each other...I want them to lose control,"* he said. *"I want to lose control. I want it to be this cathartic experience for me."*[19] After a multitude of remixes and chaotic live shows, the sound of Passions evolved into a deeper, darker outlet for hauntingly bleak post-punk explorations that evoke Cabaret Voltaire and Joy Division. Ben took further inspiration from the underground culture of 1920s Weimar Germany ("*They were so open and free artistically, almost naïve. That can't ever happen again,*" he stated), and cult films from the likes of Maya Deren's *Meshes of the Afternoon* and Kenneth Anger's *Scorpio Rising*. What resulted were songs that seemed to have been crafted in a factory, music to solder car parts to.

Ben got in a Brooklyn basement studio again for his eponymous *Passions EP* and brought Giselle M. Reiber into the project to contribute with her wonderful, brilliant voice. The EP was published on CD-R and for digital download in 2010. Five years later, a record label from Spain called Dead Wax contacted Ben to arrange a vinyl release that would include previously unpublished material. *"It's really important to me to make an album that works thematically, not just a bunch of dance tracks"* Ben asserted, trying to mentally separate his two alter egos, Math Head and Passions.

Niko Zuniga from the Dead Wax label had never got the chance to meet Ben in person, as the label is located in Spain. Only three days before Ben's passing, Ben provided the label with the final tracks for the *Passions* album.

Niko wrote afterward: *"We were shocked. Unbelievable. Ben's family and friends got in touch with us, prompted us to carry on with the vinyl release, as they knew he was really thrilled with it. Nothing could make us feel more honored than going ahead, and so we did."*

Several months after this beautiful record released, I flew to Madrid and met with Niko. As I was coming down the stairs of the hotel where I stayed and into the lobby, Niko was already there with a big package of records under his arm—meeting me, not Ben.

"We thank Ben from the bottom of our hearts for leaving us this precious gift of his talented spirit in form of the Passions album. How we wish that we could have met you face to face, Ben. Rest in peace and happiness forever." [20]

Endnotes

15. "Flâneur, from the French noun flâneur, means 'stroller', 'lounger', 'saunterer', or 'loafer'. Flânerie is the act of strolling, with all of its accompanying associations. The flâneur was, first of all, a literary type from 19th century France, essential to any picture of the streets of Paris. The word carried a set of rich associations: the man of leisure, the idler, the urban explorer, the connoisseur of the street. It was Walter Benjamin, drawing on the poetry of Charles Baudelaire, who made this figure the object of scholarly interest in the 20th century, as an emblematic archetype of urban, modern experience. Following Benjamin, the flâneur has become an important symbol for scholars, artists and writers." en.wikipedia.org/wiki/Flaneur.

16. From *Solve for Happy* by Mo Gawdat. This book about creating and maintaining happiness was written by a top Google executive after losing his son.

17. For example: "Haunting, perhaps, but nonetheless brilliant and scarily talented. Ben is one of the most dynamic and thought-provoking producers working in NYC."
    – Trashmenagerie.com; "America['s] best answer to justice." –*Dazed* (Formerly *Dazed & Confused Magazine*); and "(DEITZ) cares to push both Math Head and Passions beyond the confines of grime, dubstep, nu-rave, or any other genre tag he's currently associated with." – *Eye Weekly*

18. Passions – *Emergency*. Written by Ben Deitz. Vocals by Star Eyes. Published by Kitsuné, France, 2007.

19. From YouTube, "The Captain interviews Mathhead for Dirty Down's first installment of interviews featuring DJs, producers, and more," uploaded by Patrick Rood, Feb 12, 2007.

20. From the Passions liner notes and Dead Wax website: deadwaxrecords.es.

Time traveling

As I reminisce, I am reminded of your passion to experience every-thing that is taboo; to seek out those things that are considered offensive and immoral. Gaining access to the forbidden would take you places with intuitive thirst. At times not logical, or even rational, you would tell me "I just want to experience everything in life." You allowed the elixir of life to make you desensitized, numb, blunt, and dull. This is the place where naïveté, inno-cence, and the demons of drugs and alcohol dance together like a Sufi in the middle of his trance, or Charles Baudelaire smelling his evil flowers, as he arranges words into poetry:

> "The monsters screeching, howling, grumbling, creeping,
> In the infamous menagerie of our vices,
> There is one uglier, wickeder, more shameless!
> Although he makes no large gestures not loud cries
> He willingly would make rubbish of the earth
> And with a yawn swallow the world;
> He is Ennui—His Eye filled with an unwished-for tear,
> He dreams of scaffold while puffing at his hookah.
> You know him, reader, this exquisite monster,
> —Hypocrite reader, my likeness, —my brother!" [21]

And you? You are still so young, a teenager thrown into a private high school in NYC, beginning to detect that enticing scent: provocative yet danger-ous and delusional. You always carry with you a small notebook, writing short poems or lines inside it. Upon entering school, you write:

> I came to ██████████ school with a love of punk rock and a self-
> assured future as a writer. I had never tried very hard at school but
> could always get by well enough, especially in English and History.
> School opened me up to life in the city, particularly the life of an

uptown private school kid. Up to that point, I had spent very little time in Manhattan. On the first day in ████████████ school, I lit up a cigarette outside the school and was immediately invited to "the bench." At my previous high school, the social strata were clearly delineated. Even amongst the "alternative" youth, there were clear-cut levels of popularity. It was the prototypical hierarchy of cool and not cool. I remember visiting ████████████ school and picking out the coolest kids there and within a few months becoming their friend.

████████████ school was a reinvention of myself, one that entailed a newfound love of hip-hop, hop, drum & bass and marijuana. By the time I entered my Junior year my addiction was thriving. I was drinking in the morning and smoking weed every chance I got, as well as experimenting with everything from ketamine to ecstasy. There was an allure to drug use for me that played into the persona that I wanted to inhabit. I wanted to destroy what I perceived to be an innocent, naive child that lay inside me. There was a romance to drug use as well, and I was intelligent enough to be aware that I was playing into a stereotype, while at the same time doing little to dissuade myself from this destructive behavior. When I was 17 my drug use culminated when I overdosed on amphetamines in school and was rushed to the ER. Overdosing did nothing to dissuade me... I was then mandated to enter into an outpatient drug therapy program. Its territory became clear that I would require inpatient treatment...

It is also important to note that during this time I had my wisdom teeth removed and was prescribed painkillers. This was my first taste of opiates and I quickly realized that this was the "high" that I had always been searching for. Opiates filled the void in me that no other substance had always been searching for. This would have devastating effects on me later on later in life."

Detonated and detained.

following intense cross-examination
by fairies that fly sparkle across my view
incorporated into myth neatly wedged
between Samson and Delilah
writ infinite like petty thoughts that
repeat their rebirth endlessly
in the neuron rose bush
between our ears
thorns that draw no blood
only light that was never meant to be
and so, the waste is discarded
its use oblique and unclear
I am washed away

If ever been so precipitous,
as to merely kneel at the cliff side
I offer my incongruous font as abject evidence
that my output is still so vastly limited
that a sacrifice on my part would be wasted

White light bamboo cocktail weekend.

Enduring vinyl sunset blow job.
 Free words association fake star bullshit.

Want to smoke some weed.

Want to breath Jamaica into my lungs.
With each inhalation my soul expands,
reaches toward the dawn,
my hair grows,
I perfect myself.
Do I truly believe such?
I know not.

Exotic mushroom.

tabletop bouncer
Russian neurosurgeons
brain fucking their patients
train conductors ripping out your nails with
rusty pliers smooth skin covered delicately
and lightly with a simple fabric

Untitled. (1997)

I am buzzed.
Not drunk yet.
Even with the medication a half
A bottle won't fuck me enough. I
Prefer life intoxicated. Or I don't.
It melts the edges.
It is a light guitar strumming away.
It is sweet, I like it.

I find the following paragraph in your notes; it was probably written when you were 15 or 16 years old:

> Kierkegaard says to find commitment in life…and to stay with it, throwing away all societal norms in devotion to one's commitment. **My commitment is to have no commitment, to seize the day, to see a moment, a finite chance and to grasp it.** Perhaps that is my philosophy, Perfect spontaneity. The world would be perfect because people would take every possible chance. But perhaps people could become too vigorous and attempt to create their own chances to make events happen. I will try to flow easily, to watch as events flow past me like fish in an aquarium, and lightly and easily I will reach out and grab an event, any chance at my will. The world will flow past like an art museum, allowing me to pick and choose my thoughts and endeavors. Even my death will be an event I easily grab up when I feel it is time, or will it swallow me up? As if I was a cyclean event being picked and chosen.

Later on, you were already in your late 20s and living in Bushwick, Brooklyn, on Troutman Street. We continued to wander the new territory—it was Bushwick of 2007–08, before transforming itself into one of the trendiest neighborhoods in Brooklyn. The streets were anything but fashionable and stylish, but to our eyes, they were attractive and alive, neighbors joined together, at times just standing by or sitting on the stairs leading to their homes. Men, women, and children at all times of day; chatting, smoking, and drinking coffee from paper cups, purchased from the same corner store where we got our best sandwiches and coffee.

This neighborhood was considered to be unsafe, with an added poor reputation concerning crime and drugs. But I felt safe and protected. Ben would lead the way into some streets that were familiar to him and to some new ones. Our moving bodies brought about a new sense of openness and freedom. It liberated our jailed emotions, pausing our minds. The natural barriers between mother and son were uncovered and unmasked. "Emotions play out in the theater of the body; feelings play out in the theatre of the mind."[22]

The walls of many buildings were covered in graphic art, created illegally by ambitious and aspiring artists. To our eyes it was the natural way to

display such art, we did not need any explanation or sophisticated theories, as you wrote:

> The world will flow past like an art museum, allowing me to pick and choose my thoughts and endeavors.

I cherished that time.

Today it is called the Bushwick Collective—an outdoor gallery of graphic art, a project started and curated by Joseph Ficalora who grew up in Bushwick and is now helping to transform the place into a safe and "hip" space. He was able to obtain the permits needed to legally display artist work as well as organized tours.

Most of our outings did not have any specific aim or purpose, just toddling about, investigating or exploring streets, intimate corners, and esoteric stores that carried old books, vinyl records, and, best of all, Japanese anime, a true love of yours that would fill you up with genuine admiration for beauty and fondness for their elegant aesthetic. You reached out and grabbed them. Like you wrote: *I will try to flaw easily, to watch as events flow past me like fish in an aquarium, and lightly and easily I will reach out and grab an event, any chance at my will.* Strangers in a familiar place, we became "present absent," the city's detectives.

"Because of when I met Ben and the way in which he lived his life (through a sense of exploration) this entire city is a landscape of Ben. Corners are Ben, restaurant, parks, and train lines are Ben. Of course, this goes so much more for music and films," wrote your friend ███████ in a moving letter to us.

As we stroll through the streets of Brooklyn, you unleash your inner self, the one that has been locked inside your body for far too many years. You allow yourself to return to childhood, freedom, and energy, chatting along, shedding the rigid thickness of layers hiding your inner core. It helped me reconcile the past few years, maybe from the age of 26 to 29, when it was almost impossible for Roger and me to know what was really going on in your life and mind. At times you would say some words about your depression, anxiety, headaches, and difficulty to maintain a daily routine, but you never exposed the full expanse of your tortured self.

We were unable to help you on our own. Luckily, you would often seek out the help of a therapist, as you actually liked and believed in therapy. You also took medication at times, but not liking its side effects, you would discard

it to break free. And through it all, we were able to ignore our troubles and find these treasured times.

As we shared ideas, interests, and feelings with each other, you introduced me to the complex realms of your favorite musicians, authors, artists, and film directors; the names were mostly unfamiliar to me. My curiosity was piqued. You exposed me to Laurie Spiegel[23] and Lou Reed, his music, and his struggles with the shadowy field of gender identity, sexuality, and drugs. Your artistic endeavors also led you to admire Derek Jarmin, who you considered a "moral soul." He was a British filmmaker, artist, gardener, and a major force in the militant fight for the human rights of the gay community, long before it was tolerated, accepted, and even approved of by our society. You told me about Jim Jarmusch, the American director, who later became my favorite film director.

You invited me to go with you to see *All Lovers Left Alive*, a movie that has been ranked among the 100 greatest films of the 21st century. The dim urban scene of Detroit is set against the backdrop of Tangier, a city in northwestern

Morocco that has been at the nexus of many ancient civilizations. Vampires, addiction, depression, and music play a major role in the film, alongside allusions to literature, culture, and history. It was on a hot NYC day when the air was dense and compact. We had to part it with both hands, trying to pave the way for our bodies to move forward. Arriving into an already darkened theater, my ability to walk was compromised; I was having a hard time maneuvering the space, and Ben's hands were guiding me from behind. Again, *"Emotions play out in the theater of the body; feelings play out in the theatre of the mind."*

All three of these directors shared a strong affinity to the complexity and exploration of one's own gender and sexual identity. You were examining the same issues yourself. You shared your inner struggle openly, but somehow I have the feeling that it remained a difficult intimate matter for you to resolve. Or maybe not? I will never know. I found a short essay you wrote for English literature class at the New School. A handwritten A+ was placed on top of the first page. The paper discusses James Cameron's film *Aliens* from 1986, a science-fiction masterpiece that examines the many layers of cultural criticism during the Reagan-era United States.

You wrote:

> The inability of the male characters in *Aliens* to evolve past ancient
> gender norms leads to their deaths or, in the case of Hicks, maiming.
> ... however, *Aliens* provides a counterpoint to these stagnant males
> with the characters of Vasquez, Bishop, Newt and, most importantly,
> Ripley. These characters play with gender in varying ways, and the
> more fluidly they transgress gender roles the more apt they are
> to survive. Cameron seemed to imply that the more gender-fluid
> we are in this future, the more easily we can traverse its pitfalls
> and dangers. These characters play with gender in various ways.
> Vasquez is a woman who acts in ways that are stereotypically
> attributed to men; she is strong, talks back, speaks her mind, and is
> a warrior. Nevertheless one can possibly view her as having to act
> in a stereotypically masculine way in order to gain the respect of her
> male peers. We do not know if her way of being is natural or a coping
> mechanism in order to gain equality in a traditionally male workplace.
> In some ways, she bolsters traditional gender norms by embracing
> a one-sided view of so-called "masculinity." Her rigidity is called into
> question when she dies alongside the very men she emulates. Newt,

however, is a little girl who is not traditionally cute, but rather of androgynous physicality, which is reinforced by her genderless name.

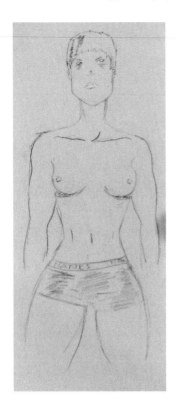

She is a survivor of trauma and precocious in ways that are generally attributed to boys. She is wise beyond her years, a strong, silent type. Bishop, while being male-bodied, is in actuality gender-neutral, being an android. It is telling that his lower half is ripped off by the queen Alien, further desexualizing him. In another light he is a safe, neutered male who has had the threat of rape removed from him. Ripley is, of course, the prime example of this gender fluidity. We can cast aside notions of masculinity and femininity with her and let her be an assemblage of characteristics and attributes rather than gender norms. She is a mother, a blue-collar worker, a trauma survivor, a warrior, a caretaker, and much more throughout the course of the film... In the ways it plays with gender, *Aliens* does much to destroy the façade of the macho, nationalistic, freedom-loving America that Reagan and Hollywood created during the 80s, all the while doing so in the very form of deliverance that was so palatable to an audience that believed in such jingoism.

One day, as we were ending our meandering walk, driving you back to your apartment, you put a disc into the CD player. It was Lou Reed singing "Oh, it's such a perfect day."

"You know, Mom," you told me, "when I went to Oregon to visit ███████. I had to rent a car from the airport and drive to her place. It was late afternoon, and I was not so sure about my driving directions. Trying to get my bearing I put this CD on, and at the same time, I was so taken by the beautiful terrain around me and the start of the sun withdrawing; I could not hold my tears back and cried quietly—it felt so good.

"I would like you to have this CD as a gift from me."

Oh, it's such a perfect day
I'm glad I spent it with you
Oh, such a perfect day
You just keep me hanging on
You just keep me hanging on

Just a perfect day
Problems all left alone
Weekenders on our own
It's such fun

Just a perfect day
You made me forget myself
I thought I was
Someone else, someone good
Oh, it's such a perfect day

I fell in love with our perfect day and with the song. "Oh, it's a love song to heroin," you tell me. And there I was, not even suspecting for a slight second how much you knew about these perfect days.

Endnotes

21. *The Flowers of Evil,* trans. Anthony Mortimer (Alma Classics, 2016)

22. From *Looking for Spinoza: Joy, Sorrow, and the Feeling Brain* by António R. Damásio (Mariner Books, 2003).

23. As before, from *Looking for Spinoza: Joy, Sorrow, and the Feeling Brain* by António R. Damásio (Mariner Books, 2003).

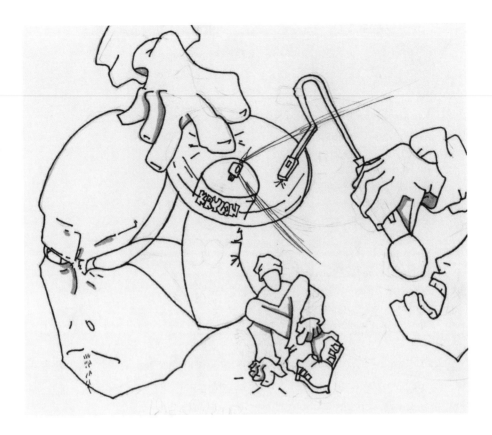

The creation of music as curative

Over 6 months after your passing, after many telephone calls from us to the coroner's office, we were able to obtain some information verbally. I did not give up and demanded a written report. I was given the address of an office in NYC. It was located in a typical high-rise building, conforming to the urban scene around it, somber and gray. Upon my arrival, after presenting my ID, I was asked to wait in the lobby. Fifteen minutes later, a young woman, probably someone from the coroner's office administration team, came out and handed me a manila envelope. The envelope contained the four typed pages of my son's autopsy report. I was asked to sign a form confirming the delivery; not a minute later, so as not to waste any work time, the young woman hurriedly departed, almost as if to escape the scene.

I left the building. Standing outside on the gray pavement, my hand clutched the manila envelope. All I wanted was to read that report, as fast as possible.

As I took a deep breath, pulling the fire of my life force deep down into my belly, my eyes scanned the pages. When I reached the end, my body craved escape—but my wings were broken, and I could not flee. Over the next few days, I embarked upon what would become a several years-long voyage. I occupied myself with the task of decoding the hidden language of medical terminology, translating minuscule measurements into less obscure ones—creating a system, a taxonomy.

An obsessive process soon found itself meandering down a twisted road, veered off from the straight and narrow. Fragments of information intersected my path, at times more confusing than helpful. A true understanding was hard to reach; I could not metabolize, whole body, what I found. I needed help from knowledgeable sources.

"Cause of death" printed in black ink appeared on top of the lifeless white paper report.

We discovered that you had a heart condition, Dilated cardiomyopathy, a condition whereby the heart becomes enlarged and cannot pump blood effectively.[24] All the known symptoms were there but went undetected. All this time, you were suffering from the compassionate fatigue of wearing your heart on your sleeve,[25] and we missed it. When we told Jay, your friend and music partner, about your heart condition, he replied: "Well, it is a perfect metaphor for Ben… He had such a huge heart."

The enormity of your heart was a burden that required many vehicles to carry it; your need for expression was central to your very being. You had always been an extremely talented storyteller, and we always assumed that you would be doing something related to writing as a career in some way, shape or form.

But as I entered sobriety (at 18) I began to experiment with making music, something that I had no prior experience with. Music was an incredible outlet for me. I loved the hard work I had to put into it to improve, and I loved every small improvement I made along the way. I would stay up until 2 or 3 in the morning every night working on songs.[26] Music quickly became my life and my love, the one thing that superseded all else. Additionally, music became a sober pursuit for me, something that I feel incredibly lucky to have found. While many musicians and artists connote their work with substance use, I have always found that substances have a deleterious effect on my work, and even while using I have avoided taking substances while making music.

I look back fondly upon these days as some of the healthiest I have ever had. My true love was music, and nothing could supersede that love. College life was also antithetical to where I was in my own life. As a sober 19-year-old who had already been living fairly independently for two years in one of the most stimulating cities in the world, I found life in the dorms to be a step back. I no longer had access to the of the city, and I was surrounded by people who were at a wholly different place in their lives than I. The primary pursuits of drugs and casual sex were of no interest to me, and I found my classes to be lacking in intellectual stimulation I moved into a loft in Bushwick with two friends. While I took a few classes and did volunteer work, I had plenty of time to focus on my true love, music. I would spend the next three years bouncing between odd jobs at coffee shops and video stores and record distributors, taking classes every now and then, and spending all of my free time making music.

Yet even your music and being sober for about 6 years from the age of 18 to 25 did not free you from deep depression, gloom, and misery. Once more you sought out narcotics for relief. In the end of February, 2013, we received a heart-wrenching letter from you, sharing with us your feelings of gloom and inadequacy, and the most terrifying words I had ever read: your admission of an addiction to opiates. Feeling powerless, you sought our help.

Without a doubt, all three of us stood firm in a fierce battle for your life. That February was a cold one. The dark winter hovered over us, and we didn't want to leave you alone, not even for a moment.

It had already been a rough season; I was sick. Really sick. I had Lyme disease, which was detected far too late. My face, ears, and head were both sore and felt paralyzed, as if an everlasting shot of Novocain was injected into me, one which did not ease the piercing pain but instead simply forced my face into a standstill position: firm, frozen and immobile. Needles were pricking my face with every gust of freezing air. And yet, I was not

troubled by it; caring for and saving you came first, and dwarfed my pain.

Every Sunday I would drive you to Brooklyn to your music studio, where you met up with Jay. "GOITIA DEITZ" you called yourself—Jay is the Goitia, you are the Deitz. "A mysterious duo from Brooklyn, New York." You were friends at heart, partners in music. Even through your suffering, you two would continue to grow, "exploring the fringes of music."[27]

As you wrote:

> "The more we played the more comfortable we got and the more we wanted to explore new elements to our sound. After many pure ambient songs, it just seemed that the logical progression was to try new elements—drums, percussion, etc. We're constantly experimenting with new sounds and ideas. When we meet in the studio there will be no plan of attack, but everything we do is written, played and recorded live, and it's vital for us to work that way. There's an immediacy and excitement to our process which is important to us and was one of the reasons we started the project. **We're not straight edge, but playing music tends to put us in a pretty meditative place, and we don't really need drugs to achieve heightened mind states.**"[28]

On the way to Brooklyn, as I drove you every Sunday to meet Jay in your studio, you were a glacial dense immovable crystal rock, which at any moment might shatter into a thousand little fragments; when I picked you up back up

Ben and Jay's studio in Brooklyn

almost two hours later, I could see that music gave you a new lease on life. You gained new energy, excitement, and strength. A new spark plug was put into your heart, delivering a new current of electricity.

Once again, music was eager to offer a helping hand. Music provided you space with no terror.

Scientists have been wondering about music's curative effects for some time. Now they are finally beginning to find some answers. Using fMRI technology, they're discovering why music can inspire such strong feelings and bind us so tightly to other people. "Music affects deep emotional centers in the brain," says Valorie

Salimpoor, a neuroscientist at McGill University who studies the brain on music. Music actually makes the brain "happy" anatomically. Distinct dopamine is released during the anticipation and experience of peak emotions that music induce.[29]

Endnotes

24. From Wikipedia: en.wikipedia.org/wiki/Heart

25. Word play on Shakespeare in *Othello:* "But I will wear my heart upon my sleeve / For daws to peck at." I.i.64–65

26. I began making music inspired by the works of DJ Shadow, who made music by sampling parts of old records to create new arrangements and songs. This method of music creation was [a help] to someone like me, who had no formal music training and could not play any instruments. While I would later teach myself how to play instruments and soon write all my music myself, I certainly would never have had the confidence to begin were it not for the art of sampling.

27. "Goitia Deitz are a mysterious duo from Brooklyn, New York. Behind the pair's shrouded persona are two DJs and producers that have been collaborating as Goitia Deitz for the past several years. 'Mode' is their follow up long playing EP to their debut EP on cut mistake 'Dream Meridian', released in 2013, which received much praise from listeners, record stores and tastemakers. Goitia Deitz have been making hybrid sounds in their Brooklyn studio for a few years now. With a pair of incredible 7s on UK based label disc error recordings championed by the likes of stone's throw records, rough trade records, & more. Their recorded experiments in minimal electronics hint towards an extensive record collection and a shared bonding over their love of krautrock, kosmische, italo, techno, and house. Nothing is pre-planned or written." Text from *Forced Exposure.* (Album produced on analog equipment, recorded live in one take with additional mixing by James Aparicio.)

28. Taken from an interview with Ben on Forced Exposure: www.forcedexposure.com/home.html

29. Dopamine is released with biological rewards, like eating and sex, for example," says Salimpoor. "It's also released with drugs that are very powerful and addictive, like cocaine or amphetamines." From "Why We Love Music" by Jill Suttie, Psy.D. in *Greater Good Magazine,* January 12, 2015.

I built an empire out of sap,
I spent years in institutions,
to realize the self does not have to be in reach

The self, as written

When your composed language unfolded onto thin white paper, you were able to discover and expose the texture of your inner self; it is an act of overpowering the silence, the one that is growing inside you. At school you are known as the best storyteller and writer. Your English teacher is proud and overjoyed, as they keep reading your writings out loud to the class or during Parents' Day in front of a much larger audience. I don't remember why but I failed to attend that Parents' Day, missing out on pride and delight. You did not even bother to tell me about it; I wonder if you got any joy out of the experience. Did it make you proud?

It should have, big time, but you remained silent.

Now that I am a mother without a child, I am free and able to read many of your stories. Getting ready to decipher your words, I can feel in my heart the blow. It feels like the wind arriving from the east, originated in the desert, scattering heavy dust all around me, and I am not able to see clearly. In Hebrew, she is called Roach[30] Kadim. "Roach" in Hebrew means spirit, as well as wind, so that is why she has the power to sweep me away, she has no pity on me. I will have to triumph over it, brush all dust from my eyes and just go on.

Reading your words is the only thing left for me, as I will never hear your voice again. These excerpts are from your high school notebooks:

> Like thin words portraying a bohemian falstitue, I crumble and spread, compress disperse like a repeat Big Bang ritual. I scream with cold rusted grasscity tunnels, melancholy returns home, encrusted eyes and aching muscles slumped gloriously in a train seat, watching the sun reflect upon dirty plastic windows, it's heavenly. Like writing myself open and softly with a pen tenderly revealing that which hurts the most. This way I fly, soaring past any flowing ending because this way it doesn't end. The pen and my life become intertwined, I live the story. And I never touch the ground again.

———————

I feel like writing. As much as James Dean felt like dying. But he had to and so do I. Don't worry I am not comparing myself to James Dean, I am not. Sometimes I wish that I could pack up and leave. I wouldn't take anything but my clothes and a couple of notepads. **I'd get in car and drive, drive, drive. I would live the way I really want to; as a roamer, seeker.** I just wanna move, far and fast, like lightning. I want to breathe in real air, and meet real people, and in a classic Ben, style has a real relationship. Zoom(?). me my cloth, notepads music (almost forgot!) and the fucking continents, I'd go to Mexico than Texas, Colorado, Washington, California, every fucking thing. I would enlist in the army, and then run cus' I know I couldn't take it. And if I ever did do that, take it as a spontaneous act of rebellion, not pre-scripted play for emotion, I'd drive, then turn around and drive back. I'd come back here and tell everyone, so I can get some attention.

Endnote

30. *Roach* in Hebrew means wind as well as spirit.

Three stories

It is about a year and a half after Ben's death and I am visiting a beautiful exhibition: a Chtchoukine collection at the "Foundation Louis Vuitton" in Paris. Standing in front of Manet's Luncheon on the Grass, the nude woman depicted in the center of the scene is not a goddess or a nymph; she is a real modern woman who took off her clothes, gazing confidently at me.

I am trying to capture every detail of the painting, but I am not able to. Next to me is a strange man pointing his full arm toward the painting while talking to a woman beside him. His arm is not blocking the view but to me it is an obstruction. I cannot take my eyes of this arm, strangely there is no gap between my body and this stranger's hand. I am uneasy and anxious, a bit lost in an unfamiliar room and very annoyed.

Slowly and miraculously, this foreign object, the strange arm, is attaching itself onto my own body. As I take a deep breath, an air of relaxation washes over me; I am able to view the picture. My body, his arm, and the picture become one. Magic is being done.

Now I am visiting another beautiful exhibition, a collection of Ben's stories. Standing in front of his notebook, tales of his life and past, the nude words of vulnerability depicted in the center of these pages, are not written by a god or a goddess; they are written by a real modern beautiful young man who took off his shield, confidently gazing at me.

This is my first time reading these stories. I try to take in every detail in every paragraph, but I am not able to. Next to me is my son, so close to my heart, pointing his full arm toward the text while talking to a lovely young woman beside him. His arm is not blocking the view, but to me it is omnipresent. I cannot take my eyes off this arm; strangely, there is no gap between my body and my son's arm. I am anxious, a bit lost in a familiar room. Slowly and miraculously, his hand attaches itself onto my body. *"You are back,"* I say softly; magic is being done.

Later, I am reading your old black notebook from middle school. You are still using only print letters. Yet you aspire to become a writer, and so you use the most impressive style and phrases at your disposal. Some of the sophisticated words are pressed firmly into the white paper, embossing the ink on top of each written letter again and again, as if to make sure that they are noticeable to the reader. A charming blend of shape and content.

Three stories written by you, at different ages, draw my attention. All of them, as I understand it, address the self. You mean a "self" that does not split the mind from the physical body; the body is not relegated to nothingness. On the contrary, you reinforce it as an essential foundation for the spirit, soul, feeling, and mind. This refined narrative of the body-mind connection is a common thread in your writing. I am not sure if you were aware of it or if your pondering mind wandered there subconsciously. You may have been drawing water from the wells of [31] the sleeping mind; but I can still remember that even as a small child of 4 – 5 years, while we were eating lobsters in Maine by the shabby gray picnic table in our garden, you made the following observation: "Lobsters are just the opposite of people." Why, we asked. "Oh, because the outside of the lobster's body is hard (shell) and protects the soft inside, and our body is soft outside (the skin) and protects the hard stuff inside (bones)." Was it just a visual observation you were making? Or already at a young age, were you staring unto the fragile material that contours and contains the physical body, not always able to guard against the hurt and pain?

Your first story, "the saxophone player," puts the physical body at the center of the plot.

The body "underpins the self," says Antonio Damasio, a professor of neuroscience, psychology, and philosophy, who investigates "why and how we emote, feel, use feelings to construct ourselves" and "how brains interact with the body to support such functions." We are not buoyant angels, but bodies that think.[32] You describe your saxophone player thusly:

> He was a man, as any other man whose sole expression and
> creativity manifested itself through a physical form, his saxophone,
> and emotion, his love for his wife Sarah.

In a different story from the same time period, you speak about the physical body and soul as they lose their unity and the self is split, not anchored. It is clear your doubts were settling in as you bring to the surface the constant inner conflict between the many opposite forces (good, evil, true, false, pleasure, pain). Occasionally, a mask covers your consciousness and reality is pushed far away. Emotional numbness takes over your body. You become the actor in a play or a movie, waiting for the director to call, "Cut!" Detachment is the name of the game. When wholeness or integration is not achieved, serenity becomes an elusive concept and a trap for self-destruction, and so it is in your stories.

At the same time, although intricate thoughts and ideas are woven into his stories, the naivety of a young man is also bursting from the text.

I assume that you are the protagonist.

I wanted to become a private eye, a detective who is willing and capable to turn grief into discovery, uncovering the hidden language of your writing and perhaps, uncovering more about your death.

I realize that when death arrives, the substance of being alive becomes elusive and is challenged beyond bounds.

Endnotes

31. Isaiah 12:3, *New International Version.* "With joy you will draw water from the wells of salvation."

32. From "The Strange Order of Things by Antonio Damasio review – why feelings are the unstoppable force" by John Banville in *The Guardian*, Feb 2, 2018.

THE SAXOPHONE PLAYER

1995, 13 YEARS OLD

Pierte was a humble man, yet he played his saxophone with as much non-conformity and existentialist angst as to himself into something akin to stream of consciousness taken physical form. He was a man, as any other man whose sole expression and creativity manifested itself through a physical form, his saxophone and an emotion, his love for his wife Sarah.

He saw her as she was, but in doing so he saw beneath her, past her, within her. He saw her slightly raised pointy ears that protrude from her dark malted hair that reached to her bony shoulders. He saw her eyes, slanted orientally, colored a dark unique blue. He saw her small lips that did not fit with the dimensions of her face.

Below them was the most perfect, rounded chin, more perfect that the most perfect circle, which did not pronounce or protrude itself astride over her other facial points but receded and melted in with her natural imperfections. It was those imperfections, those irregularities that defined and reasoned out for him his immense and deep love for her (love that I hesitate to even encroach upon you dear reader, as not to counter your own feelings on the eternal bliss).

When he looked upon her all he needed was to smile, which in turn was returned by a repeated smile from her to convey all his thoughts and conversations and emotion and other thought that would seem to fill any meaningful relationship, it was imperfections that had stirred such love within him that had kept him lovingly entwined with her (no, not married, although the term can be applied in a spiritual sense). For 17 years, his other love, his physical love which also became more spiritual, was his saxophone and the ability, no, the spiritual reasoning that allowed him to play it on the stage. While playing, it was as if he became the saxophone, cliché as it is, instead of pushing buttons he merely transmitted neural explosions that caused his creativity to bellow forth from the bellowing bronze beast which floated, suspended in his hands, or in his mind-grasp.

He would play, and play, and as if the only physical equal (of sorts) to sex he would build to a climax, and explode forth with continuous spasm of sound of jazz, of the language which stuttered out of his left brain.

And he would bow, and the crowd would be left with silence dark silence, and would attempt to fill that silence with uproarious cheers. He climbed off the stage and walked to the bar at the end of the room, and ordered coffee, and placed

his saxophone upon the bar table. And as he was drinking he turned to find his tool under artistic scrutiny by a man sketching it at the far end sitting on a red bar stool, the only one remaining of the other black ones. The artist looked upon him, and an expression came to his face, but Pietre did not understand which one it was, for perhaps it was one which he had never seen before. He found himself speaking to the artist who's expression was unfamiliar.

"My name is 'Johan,'" said Pietre.

"My name is" and the name was unfamiliar and therefore unimportant to Pietre.

"You take an interest in my saxophone, it is mine, you know."

"I realize that," spoke the artist. He had seemingly moved closer to Pietre, but was still sitting on the red stool.

It was now that Pietre realizes the artist's face. It was slightly square-jawed. His blonde hair flowed back down his head easily and his eyes seemed to be ripped from a 50-years old and placed in this 20-year-old's face. He seemingly had no lips, as his mouth clamped shut tightly.

"Why do you admire my saxophone? I would like to take it on a trip with me, as a traveling companion."

"then I shall go too."

The artist had no qualms and the two, after buying a loaf of bread, began their journey on a dusty road, surrounded by crops of the same color, outside the city. They began to walk. Several hours along the trip Pietre began to realize that with every dropping of his shoe he was killing ants. He did not know how many and so, to alleviate his pain he began to play his saxophone.

"Eventually, the artist stopped to sketch an old man by the road. As the artist sketched, the man began to disappear, until he was nothing but a blank face staring to the left on the artist's paper, "you see!" said the artist, pointing at the picture. This man was created so that I could capture him on paper. Now that his purpose is accomplished, his physical body may disappear" …

Pietro spoke to the artist: "Please sketch me."

The artist replied: "I shall draw you in phases—first, your hands."

As the artist drew Pietro's hand, it slowly disappeared, to slowly reappear upon the artist's paper. ❖

CHARLIE AND THE DOUBLE SELF

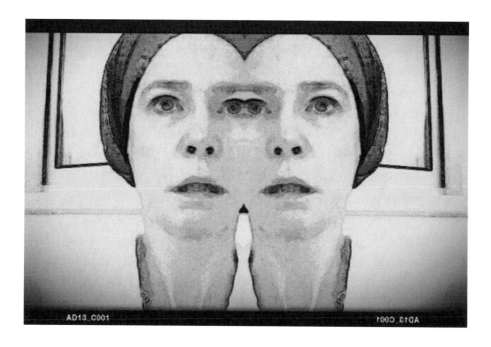

The babies jostled each other within her, and she said, 'Why is this hap-pening to me?' So, she went to inquire of the Lord. The Lord said to her, 'Two nations are in your womb, and two peoples from within you will be separated; one people will be stronger than the other, and the older will serve the younger.' When the time came for her to give birth, there were twin boys in her womb. The first to come out was red, and his whole body was like a hairy garment; so they named him Esau. After this, his brother came out, with his hand grasping Esau's heel; so he was named Jacob. Isaac was sixty years old when Rebekah gave birth to them. The boys grew up, and Esau became a skillful hunter, a man of the open country, while Jacob was content to stay at home among the tents. Isaac, who had a taste for wild game, loved Esau, but Rebekah loved Jacob.

GENESIS 25:22–27, NEW INTERNATIONAL VERSION

I had finished my deliveries and was driving aimlessly when the static of the radio broke. It was Charlie, he wanted to talk. The first time we had met was on a downtown 6 train, his confident voice punctuating the galvanized squeals of the car as he announced station stops. It was jarring. I was used to the distorted dialect of the conductors, their voices obfuscated by rusting antiquated loudspeakers. Charlie stood in pristine contrast. Particularly surprising was when he addressed me by name and told me that my fly was open. I appreciated it. I always thought it was a sign of a good friend to point out something embarrassing like that. A piece of meat stuck in your teeth, a nasty whitehead on the back of your neck. It was a kind of honesty that was rare and that I made a point of practicing. He'd made a good first impression. But then he started going off on me in a way that I wasn't too happy about. He called me a pansy, a loser. I didn't think it was fair, him berating me in front of all those strangers. I had gotten off before my stop, embarrassed. I didn't ride the subway too much after that, but my job involved a lot of driving and I learned that he too had another job: He was a news radio announcer. With that voice, it made sense. We ended up talking more often than I had ever hoped, usually on days like this, while I was trying to let the momentum of driving erase my thoughts.

"Let's talk."

"So talk."

"How was your day?"

"The usual."

"How are you?"

"Why are you asking me this?"

"Because I care?"

"You don't care. I know where this is going to end up. Just do it already."

"Okay. You're worthless."

His words sat like an oil stain in a parking garage.

I was silent for a few moments, then I forced a chuckle and an answer.

"Don't I know it."

"You don't! You're better than this, you're not even pushing yourself. You're driving around, delivering people's shit to them. People that are better than you, they amount to something. This is what you've amounted to?"

"I like this job. It keeps me from thinking. I meet people. I mean, it's easy."

"You're going to end up forgotten, dead and forgotten because you're afraid. You didn't even try."

The bottom dropped out from under me, I was weightless and worthless.

"Fuck you, Charlie."

"You're worthless!"

I laughed in agony. He joined his laugh a caustic, rusted thing.

It made me furious. I shrieked. I punched the steering wheel. I wanted to drive off the cliff edge of the road into the river below. I would be consumed, my lungs would fill and burst. My body would stay down there and my meat would be eaten by fish and I'd rot and I'd rot and I'd rot.

"You baby!" he howled back.

"I'm telling you the truth, that's all. I'm trying to help you. But I don't have to deal with your fucking bullshit!"

Charlie was gone, leaving only radio static, isolating, distant.

I had to calm down. I pulled into a parking lot by the river. I tried to force the last gasps out. My mouth tasted like dirt. I felt awful, unbelievably depressed. I tried a couple of deep breaths and then stepped out. Leaning against the hood I smoked a cigarette. I knew why his words got to me so badly. They were true. I wasn't trying very hard at life and I knew it. This was comfortable, in a way, and I had set aside my ambitions long ago. I had let myself be paralyzed by myself. There was no catharsis in this, it just built upon itself. I would fill up with all the shit and inevitably Charlie, someone, something would set it off, and I'd blow. It happened often enough. All I could do was stand and clench my thoughts uptight and try not to think, try not to breath, try not to move.

I stood smoking for a few minutes, staring at my feet. Eventually, I looked up and towards the shore. There was a girl sitting on a bench close to the water. I was drained and didn't have any anxiety left. I walked up and sat next to her, lit another cigarette and offered her one. She had short, rough brown hair, a red flannel and gray corduroys. A girl who was comfortable with herself. A smart girl. We sat smoking for a few minutes, then got to talking. Her name was X. She was clever or at the very least a good actor. She'd been sitting on that bench since sunrise, writing in a small journal about the end of the world.

"I'm trying to formulate an equation. I have a theory, and I'm trying to build it up from the foundation, like an engineer. I think that's the best way to go about these things." She spoke plainly, her eyes on the far shore of the river.

"What's your theory?"

"I think that, at the end of the world, when we all realize that it's over, like, really over, that we'll come together..." She laced her fingers together emphatically, "...in a perfect unity."

Maybe she wasn't as smart as I thought if she believed something like that.

"Huh. That's a pretty positive perspective."

"You didn't let me finish. I mean we'd unite sexually. It wouldn't be an orgy of love. It would be totally violent. Everyone would just start raping everyone. We'd all fuck ourselves to death before the end could come."

It was a clever little idea but I thought she thought too much.

"I don't think that's how it's going to be at all. We're just going to keep marching along in our routine until all the lights blink off. We're creatures of comfort, we're too scared, I think, to really make any grand gestures like that. We're too afraid."

"Maybe you're too afraid."

Yes, yes I was.

She looked me in the eyes.

"Would you rape me if the world was coming to an end?"

I thought for a while. I couldn't tell what was going on behind the static of her gray eyes. I felt that something important hinged on my answer. She was very pretty.

"Yeah, I guess I would."

She got up.

"You're fucked. You fuck!"

I felt awful for a moment but she was smiling. She sat back down, asked me a question.

"Do you want to come out tonight?"

"Where?"

"A party, in the city. We can go in now, maybe get some coffee and then we can go to this thing."

"Okay, I'll go to your party in the city."

She picked up her notebook, bottle of water, a well-thumbed copy of The Contortionist's Daughter, some pens and a cell phone and shoveled them into her bag. We got up off the bench, walked to the train station, purchased our tickets and waited on the platform, smoking.

"Do you go to school?" I asked. She was ephemeral, her attention seemed focused elsewhere, everywhere. It made me anxious.

"Sort of. Part-time I guess."

She looked me in the eyes when answering. There was a soft substance there that put me at ease.

"What are you studying?"

"Sociocultural and linguistic anthropology."

"I don't know what that means."

"It's okay. You don't have to." She looked away.

I nodded. I felt dumb but attracted to her through my idiocy.

I could feel the static start to dissipate. The indistinct shadow inside me was coagulating. I had blood in my veins. I had a heart that beat and I had a center and a self and I had a purpose. Fuck you, Charlie.

The train arrived, we got on and continued to talk. Nature encircled and embraced us, a pressure built and propelled us towards the city. Blue and green rushed by the window, became red and gray, wet paint dripping off the canvas. Water to concrete, forest to brick. Upstate New York was a thin, taut fabric that we tore away. The Bronx and then Manhattan appeared beneath.

From Grand Central, we took the 6 train downtown. A woman with a baby carriage pushed past us and onto the crowded subway car. X rolled her eyes.

"People with kids should be forced to wait until everyone else is on the train," I said.

"As punishment for procreating."

She laughed.

"I know, they should just have a separate car for them."

"Yeah, one that bursts into flames."

We sat down and I braced myself for Charlie but he was just doing his announcing routine this time. No special treatment for me.

We got off at Astor place and walked along roseate New York streets and learned about each other. We filled in the blanks of our history, making assumptions, testing intent, joking, acting dumb, smart, shy and shallow. We talked, were silent, sat on stoops, consumed cigarettes in the fading sun of a dying day. We attempted to understand and to relate, to share the memories of our brief lives. I was weightless and restless, she made me feel good. She wrote. She showed me some poems she had written, printed out and stuffed in her bag. They were good. One began with the line, mainly it's a rhythm thing.

I liked it. I took out the small notepad I kept in my back pocket and showed her a few I'd written. She read, devouring them.

"These are really good. You're better than me!"

"Thank you," I said humbly. I couldn't tell if I was being genuine or not. Hours passed.

By 11 we were online outside some bar. We went in, turned a corner and walked down into the basement. Descending, the lights faded, the walls encroached, a dark cramped void of a place. We got drinks and sat down off to the side of the dance floor. The DJ was playing something that made the speakers burst. People were packed in, delirious, dancing, sweating, screaming, smiling, posing. This was the pantomime that we resolved ourselves to. Pretending to live by going out drinking and dancing, having dinner parties, discussions, fucking and kissing, smashing our bodies into each other again and again, trying to feel. We were naive and we caused each other pain. We put masks on and tried to compose our shambling selves into something of substance. We play-acted. Sometimes we shined, but mostly we were only shallow breaths, ghosts of whispers, footprints in the mud.

I finished my drink, excused myself and got up to get another.

I watched the people move and shake, and I felt myself hollowing. I was settling into a very bad depression. Charlie was leaning against the bar, and he was speaking to me. It was the first time I'd seen him in person.

"Does it make you feel special, being this upset?"

"I don't want to hear it. I'm with a girl, she's smart, and she's pretty, and I don't want to hear it."

"She can handle herself. She's normal. More normal than you at least. I'm sure she can go out to a bar and dance and have fun like normal people do."

"This just isn't my scene. I don't feel comfortable around these people."

"Why? Are you better than them?"

"I never said that."

"But that's what you're thinking. That's your excuse. But you know what? They're better than you. All of them. By a fucking mile."

"I know. Okay? I know. I know. I know! Just let me breathe for a second. I need to breathe and I can't breathe."

"I'm not strangling you. You're broken, that's all. They probably shouldn't let broken things like you down here amongst the living."

I waited for the bartender to notice me. It took a while. I ordered a shot of whiskey and a beer, downed the shot and started sipping the beer. Charlie looked at me evenly and without emotion. People pushed past me to the bar. I was invisible.

I walked to the bathroom, beer in hand, entered a stall and closed the door. I stood sipping the beer. The muted echoes of a bass line convulsed the walls. I could hear people coming and going. Girls and boys giggled. I was a gnarled assemblage. I was rusted metal machine parts, piled and left in a dirt field in a dark wood. I could hear the cicadas and see the fireflies. It was a vision idyllic in its isolation.

Charlie was still here, though, and I could still feel him. I couldn't stay. I'd end up burning myself, or worse. I walked out to where X sat, waiting for me.

"I have to go. I can't be here. I'm going. I'm really sorry."

She looked up, concerned.

"What's wrong?"

"I think I'm having a panic attack. Thanks for today, it was lovely, really. I need to go now, though. I'm sorry."

"Okay. I don't really know what to say. I don't think you should go."

I stood there for a moment. She looked up at me, then stood. She put her arms around me and held me against her.

"It's okay."

I let go.

"I'm sorry."

She nodded, and I turned, exasperated. I couldn't do anything right. I pushed angrily past the bodies until I was outside. My face was hot and oxidized like a broken clay pot. I walked north towards Grand Central. I felt terrible for leaving X. I knew she didn't need me to be there but I felt I'd let her down. I'd let myself down. She had given me an opportunity and I had ruined it. It frustrated me. I had let myself get in the way again. I'd call her tomorrow, see if she'd give me another chance. But it was only a matter of time. Eventually, chances run out, all the options are used up, and you're left staring at a wall with nowhere to go but deeper into your own shit. In the end, maybe it was best if I didn't inflict myself on her again. I continued uptown and passed the people in their revelry. Faceless shrouds laughed and swirled. I felt alone and I felt sad and I felt cold. I walked faster. Maybe my feet would raise me up off the ground and carry me into the night. If I moved fast enough, if I concentrate hard enough, I could turn to dust and be carried off in the wind to a quiet, dark place.

I got to Grand Central. I bought a ticket to Larchmont, where my parents lived. I didn't want to spend the night in my apartment, and the thought of returning home comforted me. I went down to the food court. There was a small Indian food stand, but all the customers had skipped it to eat at the adjacent pizza shop. My heart broke a little for whoever owned the Indian place, but not enough to eat there. I bought two slices and sat down and ate. I felt more whole there then I had ever felt at any bar or club or party. Here amongst the remaining few leaving the city, the last drops of blood being squeezed from a pinprick wound. I wanted to separate from everything and disappear. To be unmade, remade. A paper-thin ghost, a page of newspaper being blown in the wind. When had things become so complicated, so caked and brittle? How can so much shit just pile on? It was always accumulating. Every decision was a mistake, every move the wrong one. I bought a pack of cigarettes and went outside and smoked one.

The train ride made me feel better, the momentum began to heal me. I wished I would never arrive. Heaven would be an endless journey with no destination. No home to go to, no pain to run from. Staring out the window, I watched my reflection merge with the passing lights and shadows, fading and reconstituting with the restless landscape. In the passing buildings, my eyes were cast in the dimmed lamps that shone behind drawn curtains. I was not looking at myself, I was not looking at the city outside. I wanted X to be sitting beside me. I wanted to rest my head on her shoulder as we careened through this quiet night.

I arrived, the train departed, and I was left alone on the platform. There was a purity and a stillness in the atmosphere. I walked home past a landscape charged with the subdued tension of memory. Every bowed tree and cracked piece of concrete sidewalk was saturated with a melancholy remembrance. All my memories of young love, inebriation, laughter, fights, beer, weed, saliva, and cough syrup. Here lay youthful exuberance, dormant in elementary school playgrounds and worn park benches. All my essence had shed this stalking husk of a body and permeated into the soil. It had left me.

I got home, there were no cars parked in the driveway, my parents weren't there. I went around the back, found the key hidden on the porch and let myself in. I dropped my body onto the sofa and sat for a few minutes, breathing. The house was quiet and still, illuminated by the petrified light of the moon. I took my clothes off, laid down on the couch, covered myself with a blanket and closed my eyes. I could hear the muted echoes of the highway in the distance. My mind ached from thought. All I could do was lay there and stew in it until it became unbearable, then shut off. Eyes closed, listening. The moonlight resting heavily on my eyelids, the faraway highway drone, the weight of it all pressing down on me like a veil, waiting for it to pass, waiting for the blunt trauma of existence to knock me out, waiting for the void. Waiting, I slept.

And then I awoke. I wasn't sure what time it was. I forced myself off the couch and padded groggily into the kitchen, put the kettle on the stove. The day looked warm and the sun beamed through the windows in anticipation. I put my clothes on, sat back down on the couch and wrote a poem down in my notebook: A capitalistic endeavor ends in a car crash.

I tore the page from the notebook and went out onto the back porch, walked into the backyard and dug up a small hole in the dirt with my hands. I placed the paper in the hole and refilled it, then stopped. I looked around, wondering if anyone had seen me. All of a sudden the foolishness of my gesture hit me, and I hurried back into the safety of the house. In my periphery I saw Charlie standing underneath a tree, laughing.

I made myself a cup of tea, drank half of it, brushed my teeth and washed my face, put my shoes on and stepped outside. I started walking into town. I passed the elementary school playground and the air filled with the choral din of children playing. I lit a cigarette and walked faster. ❖

DETACHMENT FROM THE PHYSICAL BODY

10:30 PM   **Ben:** hey man![33]

10:31 PM   what's good

10:32 PM   —nothing

                      —just you know

                      —still setting shit up

10:42 PM   **Ben:** haircut

    sending a new story to some literary mags

    people say it will probs get published

    hope theyre right

11:01 PM   **Ben:** yo

11:02 PM   how was your week

                    —your's?

11:03 PM   **Ben:** intense

11:04 PM   **Ben:** yeah lot of stuff came up in therapy

    intense stuff

    that i have to deal with

11:05 PM   but its for da best

    Ben: no like

    Ben: stuff that happened to me when i was younger,

    and these out of body experiences i have,

    and how they tie in with extreme behavior as an adult

    Ben: lol

11:07 PM   —ku-kuro

                    —Kurio

11:08 PM   **Ben:** yeah

    i just never thought it was relevant

Endnote

33. Text from a chat session between Ben and his friend

I am able to recognize these same sensations you are describing, in a distinct memory from my childhood that is etched into my mind. A group of children from my class did not want to accept me into their crowd and asked me not to join them for a weekend outing. Standing there by myself a short distance away I felt rejected and hurt to the very core of my being. I experienced the feeling of being alienated from any physical surroundings that encapsulated me. My body disappeared into numbness; only my eyes kept gazing into the distance.

This occurred once in my adulthood as well.

I don't know all of your journeys, Ben, but I have traveled some of the same roads.

Photo by Sara Lemieux

UNTITLED STORY

Florian emerges from a darkened corridor into the living room and sits on the couch. "Sorry, I had some business to take care of." He says. He lights a cigarette and for a moment his body blurs, subtly, shimmering darkly as the tobacco and paper starts to burn. For that brief second, he's there but not there, like some terrible thing glimpsed peripherally in the shadows. He takes a loud, caustic drag and comes back into focus. He winks at me and takes an iPhone out of his breast pocket. "Check this out." He says as his fingers slide across its surface. He holds the phone up to my face and on its screen is the digitally obfuscated image of a CCTV camera. I can dimly make out a recessed stairwell and trash bins and the overblown patina of a sodium-vapor lamp. It's the sort of pixelated video you see on TV when they show convenience stores being robbed on shows like "Caught in the Act." Staring at it I suddenly realize that the feed is coming from atop the front door to Florian's apartment building, and the concurrent stimuli of the immediate, internal surroundings of the apartment and the world directly outside of it produces a weirdly dissociative effect. My brain reels and I blink and rub my eyes.

"I just got done setting the last one," Florian says.

"That's smart, in case someone tries to break in or whatever."

"Yeah I've got one in every room now. All the feeds are hooked up to my phone, so I can monitor the house at any time, from anywhere."

He presses the corner of the screen and the images change, cycling through each feed. There are seven cameras, located throughout the apartment and the building's exterior. The silent images are clinical and distant, like watching a degraded VHS tape of a dream you can barely remember, washed out and foreign and deeply, deeply unsettling. "I gotta girl moving in next week, into the back room." He says lasciviously. I think that I should laugh in response but I'm too busy scanning the ceiling, unable to locate the living room camera. It films me as I put a cigarette to my lips, films Florian as he languidly leans over, his shirt cuff pulling back from his wrist to reveal a gold watch, his hand lightly holding a Hermes lighter. He lights my cigarette and I lean back into the couch, inhaling and exhaling, eyes upward and scanning. Florian turns on the TV and starts watching a movie that I can't pay attention to.

Later on, after I feel I've worn out my welcome I step outside to start home. I stop to light a cigarette and look around at the scene I'd been watching earlier on Florian's phone, all the details lost in the grainy, silent footage of his security

camera. It's rained briefly and the night has been left drained and collapsed in spo-
radic puddles along the sidewalk. I hear a dog bark ricochet off the nearby apartment buildings and the muted echo of a police siren howls like a dying animal in
some far off wood. The sodium-vapor lamp casts a flickering spotlight upon me.
I can feel the indifferent lens of the camera. I feel it in the way my posture stiffens,
in the way I self-consciously lift my cigarette to my lips and slowly inhale, in the
way I nervously shift my weight from left to right foot. I am the entertainment
now. I am the actor, portraying a two-dimensional ghost of myself. The street is
a poorly constructed sound stage, the buildings behind me are thin fabrications
of polystyrene and plywood. The dog barks and the police sirens and the ambient
street noise are pre-recorded stock sound effects. An extra shuffles briefly into the
foreground of the frame, pushing a red grocery cart filled with cans. I finish my
cigarette and exit the scene. ❖

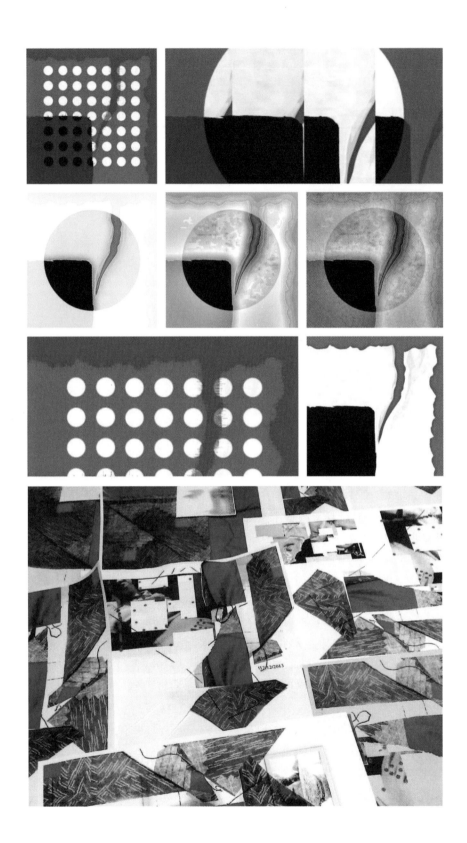

Art by Chagit Deitz

Scrapbooking

As a child, I had a favorite ritual. Every Friday I would visit the local shopping center in the small neighborhood where I lived. An old man with a snack cart would sell candies, sunflower seeds, and Krembo.[34] We used to call him "Peanuts and Seeds." He came to our small neighborhood, pushing a cart all the way from a distant modest town. He would wrap the seeds in a cone made of old newspapers. My weekly allowance would be quickly spent on his goods, which would keep me company while I read. Food and books were my favorite combination: I should have named it texfood. My next stop was visiting Mrs. Cain's. She had a small lending "library" in the rear corner of her stationery store, and charged a small fee for borrowing books. We did not have a local public library or one within our small school; thus, Mrs. Cain's was my go-to.

Mrs. Cain was a lovely woman, a Holocaust survivor from Hungary. She was a "comrade" of my mother's; each carried a blue tattoo on their arm, and both were always inspecting my collection. Luckily, I was interested in Holocaust books for children (yes, there is such a genre), detective books written by Agatha Christie, and the Russian novelist, Lydia A. Charskaya, (most of her stories deal with young girls in a boarding school. The protagonists were usually independent girls looking for adventures). The Holocaust-themed books' endings were invariably bad ones; whereas, the detective genre rescued my soul by promising that justice, morality, and a happy ending will prevail.

Life events resemble an intricate communication system, a network of individual threads that overlap and form a webbed whole. As time passes, single isolated threads lengthen, merge with others, and become the basic life material that intertwines into a larger cloth. The thin cord that was put through the needle and solidified within me the tradition of reading books is woven through all my patterns. My family gave reading a prominent role in their lives; my parents' home, as well as my grandparents' home, were full of books. Many libraries filled them; each shelf contained rows and rows of books, in double rows.

Our library at home follows this tradition. So did Ben's.

After Ben's tragic passing, I had an immense need to connect myself to everything that was a part of his life. I visited our summer home in Maine, where we kept Ben's ancient comic books from his childhood, and I could not stop staring at them; they were everywhere around. There was nowhere to escape from memories that made my eyes tear up.

I could not resist reading some of them. It has always been hard, even impossible for me to "get" and value comics. I am patently unable to strike a match and light a candle between the text and the visual art. That kind of orientation in space was too confusing for me. Ben used to make fun of my comic illiteracy and did not concern himself with the business of clarification. I have to confess, I was never truly interested. But now, circumstances and desires have changed, and upon re-encountering Ben's collection, I became fascinated by their art and content.

Most of Ben's comics addressed the journey of a hero. If my existence is compared to Penelope's, his mirrored Odysseus, leader of the Trojan War, king of Ithaca, who fights his way to create a home for his soul. Constant moral and physical challenges confront him. The hero has to work through these obstacles in unfamiliar territories. He does not always find his wings.

Blending the verbal with the visual, comics were a space so close to Ben's heart; a few words that convey the most valuable messages. Young and impressionable, and identifying with the main characters, comics became another path to expression for Ben—an alternative road upon which he never ceased traveling during his short journey.

As Spiderman learned the hard way, "With great power, there must also come great responsibility."[35]

Only later would I discover the deep connection between Ben's world and mine; yet, I have never traversed the short road between the power of life, imagination, and death.

Even before you read comics, you watched cartoons.

You are 5 years old. Every morning before school you love to watch G.I. Joe on TV. The show allows you to come up with imaginative new ways of playing with your action figures. But you have been forbidden from bringing your action figures to school, and at the same time, I was asked by your teacher not to let you watch this show before school. It made you "wild," she claimed. Instead, I let you watch some programs about nature. And yet: Isn't being wild a part of nature? I thought so myself, but never expressed it out loud.

Eventually, watching TV before school was stopped, but not even your teacher could ban your imagination.

Your report card tells us:

> "Ben is an enthusiastic, outgoing bright energetic child. He loves coming to school and had no problem integrating into kindergarten. He is a self-starter, highly motivated, and always has a unique way to complete a project. for example, one day he took several pieces of paper and was cutting and pasting and singing all morning. When he left the room for lunch, he showed me a life-size paper robot he named "Mikey." He told me he would have a friend to play with all afternoon."

My mother used to keep all of my old notebooks, letters and drawings from when I was very young. Every visit to my parents' home involved a ritual of a past remembrance, taking former life events prisoner, holding them in the cell of my mind.

Too often, I refused to let go: I would stare for hours at old family photos, pore over my drawings from childhood; they were funny and naïve. I read my early poems. Some of them were copied from famous poems; I did not think that anyone would be able to tell the difference. Again, naivete prevailed. My mother lost everything from her past once, and she was not going to let it happen again. And now, I follow suit.

Sarah Kofman, a distinguished philosopher recounts her personal memories in a short book titled: *RUE ORDENER, RUE LABAT*. It is her only piece of personal writing telling her story as a young Jew in France during the second world war. In this private and revealing journey, she depicts her emotional saga and tragedy of being torn between her own mother and the woman who hid her, MÇmÇ, the woman who she loved and cherished. Kofman committed suicide in 1994. She was 60 years old.

All that she retained after the war was her father's fountain pen:

> "Of him, all I have left is a fountain pen. I took it one day from my mother's purse, where she kept it along with some other souvenirs of my father. It is a kind of pen no longer made, the kind you have to fill with ink. I used it all through school. It 'failed' me before I could bring myself to give it up. I still have it, patched up with Scotch tape; it is right in front of me on my desk and makes me write, write. Maybe all my books have been the detours required to bring me to write about that."

I followed my mother's tradition without hesitation and treasured every piece of paper from your childhood. Most of your writings and paintings from an early age are carefully kept in the attic. Actually, it is a third floor that had been converted into a playroom, a space just above your bedroom, the two connected with a private staircase. When you shut the door to your bedroom, all this space turned into your own private chamber and domain, separated from the rest of the house. A place where you glowed, dreamed, shed tears, kissed your first girlfriend, got drunk, and chain-smoked—always remembering to keep the window open.

Your very first story was written at the age of 5 or 6. You brought it to life with a charming drawing:

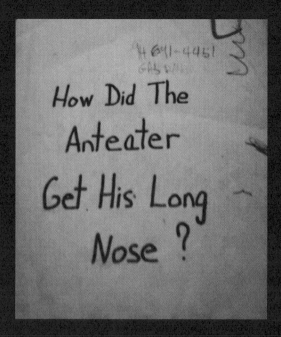

How Did The Anteater Get His Long Nose?

Once upon a time, there was a gerbil that lived far away on a little island.
And there was a bull that lived on the island.
One day the bull chased the gerbil far into the island, where he had ever been.
And he came to a big mountain,
Where god lived.
And the gerbil said to the god "I want to be much bigger,
so I can run away from the bull and he will not catch me."
The next day he was a little bigger
Every day he got a little bigger
His nose got longer too.
He said to himself, "I don't want this long nose
I cannot eat grass."
But he had to live with it.
He was very hungry.
When he was a little gerbil
He remembered seeing ants.
Ah, now with his long nose
he can smell them.
And he is going to sniff
Them on the ground
And gobbled them up.

Five years old, and already you were discussing the lack of contentment in being small and weak. Indeed, the gerbil is small compared to the hefty and strong bull. For a moment you stretch the drama, and the reader prepares to witness the bull attacking the helpless gerbil. You allow the reader to worry... but then, there is a sudden shift in the plot: The bull starts to chase the gerbil, but in the midst of his charge, new opportunities arise. The gerbil finds himself in a place unknown to him, upon a towering mountain, where he finds... GOD! The overseer of the universe, an omnipotent God, "He"[36] has the ability and power to accomplish all.

God's power is unlimited. In the illustration, you gave him 4 hands, and he indeed stretches out his hand to help. *Behold, the LORD'S hand is not shortened, that it cannot save; neither his ear heavy, that it cannot hear.*[37]

where a God lived.

The four hands of god [43]

Each one of your stories that has elements of a fable likewise ends up with a lesson and a moral: Everything in life has a price, make the best out of it; when having a very long nose, the gerbil was able to *smell them* (the ants). *And he is going to sniff Them on the ground And gobbled them up.*

Days and years are moving quickly. You are in your teens and older, and do not cease from reading and writing graphic novels, but you add new materials: your bookshelves, and notebooks for your writing. Actually, there was no need for new notebooks, as a laptop alongside your school notebooks become the perfect space for your writing. I have to admit that I did not come across a single word or number related to schoolwork in any of your notebooks. I am not surprised.

Instead, heroic plots, thoughts about your existence, and poetry full of desire, horror, and hearty illustration are what I found. They are like a blueprint for each period of your boyhood and youth. Your soul is yearning, asking: what? why? and how.

A storm of emotions was seeking a way out.

I look around your room. The bookshelves are loaded, following our family tradition. New books excite your imagination: the dark apocalyptic novels by Cormac McCarthy; Kafka, the storyteller with his bizarre fantasy tainted with self-abasement, detached from his body, claiming: *What have I in common with the Jews? I have hardly anything in common with myself;*[38] Howard Phillips Lovecraft, who utilized the concepts of the uncanny and the bizarre, and allowed eerie events to take place.[39] There are more: The Scottish writer Iain Banks, who wrote a horror story about a psychopathic teenager living on a remote Scottish island. William Faulkner, Anais Nin, Tim Power, and William Gay Scott are all consumed by you. They all have one thing in common: They are somber, dark, dealing with the end of life and the obscure.

WB Yeats, the Irish poet, and writer, left a particularly profound impression on you:

> To fully understand Yeats's work, one must understand his fascination with the supernatural and the unexplained. While many of Yeats's works deal directly with ideas of mythology, magic and the supernatural, those that do not directly address these issues nevertheless use imagery that is drawn from a lifetime spent in the study of the unknown. The idea of the supernatural became tangible in the countryside of Sligo, where any number of mythical creatures and occurrences could be waiting just around the corner, and where Yeats claimed to have seen his first fairy, sliding down a moonbeam. This corporeal idea of the mystical presents itself in many of Yeats's poems, such as "The Stolen Child." In this poem, faeries attempt to lure a child away from the comforts of a normal earthly life with promises of "vats full of berries," "olden dances," and other wondrous things. The poem has its roots in Irish folklore and the belief that faeries could steal children away to be their companions, and specific references to the Sligo countryside give one the impression that Yeats must have felt the call of the faeries during his childhood there. While Yeats himself could be seen as the tempted child, it could also represent his brother Robert, who died in Sligo when he was three years old. Perhaps Yeats was fancifully positing that Robert was merely lured away by a mystical creature.

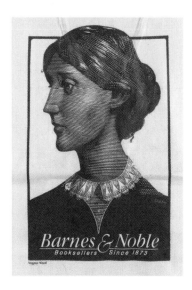

A memory springs to my mind while looking around your room: Mother and child, chit-chatting at Barnes and Noble. You are 5 or 6 years old.

"*Mom,* look up, at the picture on the wall, do you see the woman who put her head in the stove?"

"No, son, this is the woman who put rocks in her pocket."

Endnotes

34. *Krembo* is the name of a chocolate-coated marshmallow treat that is popular in Israel.

35. The Peter Parker principle, a proverb popularized by the Spider-Man comic books written by Stan Lee.

36. For the sake of simplifying my writing, I refer to God as a male—as used in male terms in Biblical sources. [Citation in original]

37. Isaiah 59:1, King James Version.

38. The teacher wrote under the drawing "Where a God" to correct Ben. But the dictionary definition is the following: "A god is a supreme being or deity, and it's spelled with a lowercase g when you're not referring to the God of Christian, Jewish, or Muslim tradition. The ancient Greeks had many gods — including Zeus, Apollo, and Poseidon. A physical representation of a deity is also called a god." Source: vocabulary.com

39. Quote excerpted from *He: Shorter Writings of Franz Kafka,* edited by Joshua Cohen, riverrun editions, 2020.

40. Expanding on [Freud's] idea [of the uncanny], psychoanalytic theorist Jacques Lacan wrote that the uncanny places us "in the field where we do not know how to distinguish bad and good, pleasure from displeasure" resulting in an irreducible anxiety that gestures to the REAL. (Source: Wikipedia)

David Foster Wallace

"right now, I want to be anyone but me anywhere but here anytime but now. There isn't a sound in the world that will drown this feeling out. Not a sound"

– FROM A HIGH SCHOOL NOTEBOOK

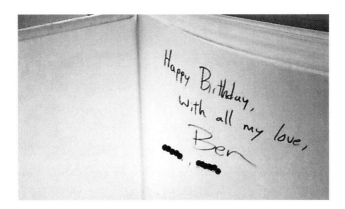

For my 60th birthday, you traveled to Israel for a small birthday celebration with my family. You brought me a lovely gift, a small book, carefully wrapped in white tissue paper. It was called *This is Water*, and was the Commencement speech given to the Kenyon College graduating class of 2005, written and read by David Foster Wallace, probably the most acclaimed writer of his generation.

On May 17, 2016, *Literary Hub* published an essay titled: "How the Best Commencement Speech of All Time Was Bad for Literature," written by Emily Harnett. A bit of an awkward title for a complimentary review, but she goes on to clarify:

"This is Water is the best commencement speech of all time," not because it outdid the formula of any other speech, but because it used the time-honored traditions more effectively. The speech begins with an ordinary, even a bit tedious, account: Two young fish are swimming together as they happen to meet an older fish swimming in the opposite direction; "How is the water?" he

asks. The young fish continue to swim quietly, and then all of a sudden one of them looks at the other fish and goes: "What the hell is water?"

Indeed, the most obvious facts are often ignored. They are the hardest to see. The speech goes on to remind us all of the most important lesson in life: The fact is that in the daily routine of life (Foster calls it the "trenches of adult existence"...) banality can hide the real value of learning. "It has nothing to do" with information, data or knowledge, but it has everything to do with simple awareness; "awareness of what is so real and essential, so hidden in plain sight all around us, all the time, that we have to keep reminding ourselves over and over:

"This is water. This is water."[40]

This was not the first time that I had come across David Wallace Foster's name and writing. In August 2004, I read "Consider the Lobster." It was published by *Gourmet Magazine,* a magazine known for allowing the space for vanity and the good life. It was printed on fancy glossy paper, hidden behind pretentious photos and advertisement. Wallace had visited The Maine Lobster Festival in Camden, Maine, one of Maine's nationally renowned premier summer events. He was not there to devour a good meal for a cheap price, nor to suggest a new recipe to his readers. He was there to debate some disturbing matters: Is it OK to boil a living alert flesh and blood creature solely for our gustatory pleasure?

I cherished the essay but did not bother to search for other books written by Wallace. When you surprised me with *This is Water*, I was delighted. You knew where and how to aim into my heart and taste.

I think of David Foster Wallace as the "continental divide" between your generation and mine: 16 years younger than myself and 16 years older than you.

Placing himself high above events as they unfold, Wallace had a very particular conception of the future: loneliness, disconnect, drugs, alcohol, and depression are some of the many instruments that played in his orchestra.

I am not surprised that you thought of DFW as your "comrade"; you worshipped him. For you, he was not only a literary genius, the author of *Infinite Jest,*[41] but also the quintessential tormented artist—a man trapped in negative thoughts about the self, ever-focused on the dissonance between the hidden inner life and the exposed, barren outer one.

You both had a disposition that barred integration between the many virtues any one person possesses: evil and good; honesty and dishonesty; fake affect and authenticity; sadness and happiness; loyalty and betrayal, and so much more.

When I think of any literary attempt, known to me, to translate depression into the printed medium, *Infinite Jest* is the first and only time that I have begun to believe or trust in humankind's ability to provide a "blow-by-blow" account of depression.

David Foster Wallace did not look for a rare or exotic explanation for his suffering. He stayed within his own familiar terrain, the obvious one that omits the trivial question "What the hell is water?" or "What the hell is depression?" He simply dwells there: *This is depression. This is depression.*

"... It's a kind of spiritual torpor in which one loses the ability to feel pleasure or attachment to things formerly important ....The anhedonic can still speak about happiness and meaning et al., but she has become incapable of feeling anything in them, of understanding anything about them, of hoping anything about them, or of believing them to exist as anything more than concepts.... It is also lonely on a level that cannot be conveyed .... It is a hell for one.... The person in whom *Its* invisible agony reaches a certain unendurable level will kill herself the same way a trapped person will eventually jump from the window of a burning high-rise. Make no mistake about people who leap from burning windows. Their terror of falling from a great height is still just as great as it would be..."

– DAVID FOSTER WALLACE

"I've also experienced the depth of depression and anxiety. I've spent years suffering from utter anhedonia, wishing I was dead, consumed by total self-loathing."

———————

"It is like I am dragging these lives with me a boulder on my back throughout life. Just want a body and a drink and some hope, something to search for..."

———————

"False childhood upbringing, quick spasmatic purge ejaculation. If you read this, I grow horns. I am a tumor growing in my attic brain, I'm melting and evaporating like frying porridge on an emaciated trenchcoat body

don't want to

Think

Breath

Blink

Defecate

Starve

Go insane (I am afraid...I don't want to lose my mind)

Be afraid

Stink

Sink

Anymore"

———————

"This fear won't leave. I don't know what of, Filling me with utter hopeless and purely awful fear of the here, the now, and the then."

At the tender age of 13, Ben wrote a compassionate short story called "Coliseum—the story of Raymond." It was handwritten in one of his class notebooks. Some segments of this story are germane, and I am including them here:

>...Raymond took his seat with hurried anticipation. The show was about to begin. He sat down in the cold blue plastic "seat" and watched the spectacle unfold before him. The coliseum was a circular arena. There were two levels, the upper of which Raymond sat in. Each row of seats was elevated slightly from the proceeding row in front of it. Many of the seats around Raymond, in fact almost all of them, were empty. Raymond took [note] of this, realizing that it would make an uncomfortable situation if he had seen the day events and his friends and family had not. He stood up to leave but knocked his head (quite forcefully enough to send blood flowing from his nostrils), against the nothingness before his seat. He turned to face his seat, holding his head as it leaned forward to rest against the seat. Instead it again (not quite as forcefully) knocked against the nothingness that was behind his seat. He reached his hands out to feel the invisible barrier to his left and right. What was this? He was boxed in like an animal, boxed in between walls of...glass. It was glass that held him prisoner! He forced his arms to push against the left and right walls so as to lift his legs up and kick them against the glass. In the row behind Raymond, the row raised a little higher than his own, sat two rotund men, whether Raymond saw them or not they did not know. The two had lengthy, waxed mustaches that painted out from their faces, large top hats and grayish brown business suits, they looked upon him with an air of indifference, not as men looking upon a caged animal but as scientists studying some peculiar happening. One of the men spoke, though which was hard to tell.

>"What a poor pity" the other answered.

>Raymond continued to beat up on the glass walls in apparent vain, when, in despair, he looked up to see the sun poking out from behind its clouded hideaway, a bird perhaps a seagull, Raymond did not know, swooped down into his glass cage. Raymond looked up, there

was no glass covering the top of his cage. He attempted to climb up, but the higher he went the taller the walls grew until he dropped down and sat slumped in his chair....

Soon the days rolled by, Raymond grew strong and healthy... It was a bright day, the sun ducking in and out of the cover of clouds, birds singing their incessant songs when the walls lifted. Raymond did not hear them move, but he was sitting on his chair when he felt a strong gust of wind. He knew something was amiss. He stood up and took one cautionary step forward then another then stepped out of the confines of his invisible cage...he took another slow step away from his seat and was suddenly aware of an acute sense of longing and sickness. Each step he took made him sicker and sicker until he felt that the pit of his stomach had shrunk to the size of a peanut. He dropped to his knees, looking toward the sky in desperation, then threw up upon the stone floor. This relieved no pain or suffering, and so Raymond turned around... ❖

Make no mistake, the trapped person in a cage will eventually escape but their terror of the outside world will capture them just as well.

David Foster Wallace was prescribed antidepressants and resented it. At times Ben would blame me for "pushing" medication on him. "I don't know who the real Ben is anymore" was your argument. Foster was a dedicated member of an AA group in Boston, and you were a devoted and loyal member of such a group in NYC. Wallace wanted to excel at everything that he touched and to be a "good" person. He developed an inner conflict, split between his yearning for recognition and his inner fear of being a "fake," as his protagonist Neal describes himself in Wallace's story, "Good Old Neon."[42] David Foster Wallace took his own life at the age of 46. Despite identifying with Wallace, you did not lose the ability to recognize your own voice and tonal expression:

I judge artistic endeavors based on how deeply they stir my emotions. A work that can bring me to tears is a successful piece of art because it has honestly communicated something between its creator and its audience. The work itself becomes a commonality between people despite the disparities of the individual and the fundamentally isolating nature of subjective perception. The short

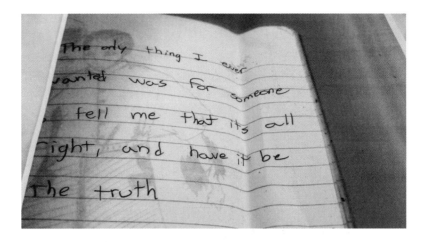

story "Good Old Neon" by David Foster Wallace not only achieved
this but did so through a meta-textual examination of the act of
communication itself. Very few works of art have so exposed truth
of humanity so precisely and poignantly to me, and so profoundly
altered how I perceive myself and my own life.

The story's narrator intricately recounts his lifelong struggle with an
emptiness of self, culminating in his suicide. We learn of the moment
he realizes his fraudulent nature, the calculated persona he adopts in
relation to others, his preparation for and eventual suicide, and finally
the clarity he acquires in an afterlife that exists outside the confines
of time. As the meticulous complexity of the tale is unraveled, it
becomes a meditation on the inadequacy of language to express the
depths of our inner being. The narrator realizes the impossibility of
having an honest relationship to others when trying to express the
totality of a self through the limitations of language is like trying to
"see each other through... tiny keyholes." The culmination of the story
brings Wallace himself in as a participant, and calls into question
whether he has written this as a rumination on a classmate's death,
or perhaps merely an exhaustive examination of his own struggles
to express himself adequately. "Good Old Neon" is not only an
example of astonishing craft and intellect, but also a deeply moving
meditation on the human condition. It has influenced me as an artist,
inspiring me to improve the depth of what I hope to express, and
influenced me as a human being, causing me to examine how I relate
to others and to myself."

"Everything that slows us down and forces patience, everything that sets us back into the slow circles of nature, is a help. Gardening is an instrument of grace."

MAY SARTON

Every summer when I am in Maine, I dig into the earth. I remove weeds, prune dead branches and plants from the earth, thin abundant flower beds, and plant new one, hoping for them to come back after the harsh winter. Ben is here with me; the perennial flower that will continue to bloom year after year—forever and a day.

At times, when serenity and pleasure are taken away from me, I cannot help but visualize depression as a tool, a real one. It is the shovel that I use, the one that digs itself into the ground deeper and deeper toward the abyss. You never held back any words trying to dig into the nature of depression.

Endnotes

41. Taken from DFW's *"This Is Water: Some Thoughts, Delivered on a Significant Occasion, About Living a Compassionate Life"* commencement address given in 2005 at Kenyon College.

42. *Infinite Jest* is a 1996 novel by David Foster Wallace.

43. "Good Old Neon" was originally published just three months after the 9/11 terrorist attacks.

I keep picking
at the melted wax
that's run down my cheeks
until I realized
that it's just dried tears.
I've been crying all evening
over ruined things

———————————

I saw a man
get a pizza knocked out of his hand
by some teenagers
he was stunned
ruined
I imagine him returning to his wife
and being cradled in her arms
as he sobbed out a ruined evening

Art by Chagit Deitz

Traveling to Louisiana

TRAVELOGUE/MINI-MEMOIR BY BEN, MID-20s

There is a secret place I go to when I am in pain. I discovered it in London, dressed in white and lying on a friend's bed, trying to get through a stupid agony I put myself into. It is a beach, somewhere south, and I lay on it, naked and alone, as the waves break calmly against the shore. Here, I am at ease. One day I hope to find my way to this isolated shore, and imprint myself upon the sand, and be swept into the whole and good and lovely nothingness.

Things go wrong in myriad ways. And maybe, eventually, you get so tired of putting all the pieces back together again, that you let them lay there, their brutal clarity staring back at you like a wound. I decided to go to Louisiana and give something of myself. The decision may have been borne out of desperation, a frantic clawing and flailing of limbs, an attempt to somehow escape myself. Maybe it was just a lazy shrug, maybe it wasn't much at all. As I prepare to catch a couple hours of sleep before a 7 AM flight to New Orleans, I find myself fighting back small bouts of tears.

The cab driver takes me to the airport through a New York that has warped and grown overnight; I've never seen it before. At 5 AM, post-rain, pre-dawn, past verdant parks and lush overgrowth, dim halogen glows beneath highway overpasses, a tropical overgrowth has consumed the city and made it purple green and new. I arrive in New Orleans and in a taxi to the Amtrak station we pass a cemetery whose inhabitants have chosen exclusively to reside in mausoleums. These intimate cathedrals, some ornate, some simple, like a somber marble slum.

In the Amtrak station. There is a badly sunburnt teenager sitting in front of me in the waiting area. He has his shirt lifted over his back and a stout woman in green is rubbing suntan lotion on his back, apologizing every few minutes. "I'm so sorry, I'm sorry." I realize that she is not his mother and that they may have just met. Near the bathrooms, a young woman weighs herself on a pay-to-use scale. I buy a sandwich at a Subway. The radio is blasting and I keep thinking I hear someone singing along to it but can see no one. The accompaniment becomes louder and louder. There is a gambling booth in the corner, with raised walls like a bathroom stall and batwing saloon doors like the adult section of a video store. The signs say you must be 18 to enter and 21 to gamble. A man exits through the saloon doors and I realize he's the one who's been singing.

On the train, heading to Schriever (I pronounce it "*shry*-ver" at first, but it's "*shree*-ver"). The conductor almost shouts the name out when he takes my ticket. I can't tell if he's shocked or confused at my destination. Outside the window I see two birds fly low over the ground, but one just keeps circling and I realize it's a plastic bag. All the trees are bowed and resigned, lurching, poor postured shrouds that seem about to collapse like drunks into the clearing around the tracks. The air is filled with dandelion clocks, plankton viewed through the fogged porthole of a deep-sea submersible. I read the last lines of a Bukowski poem:

> *they feel no terror*
> *at not loving*
> *or at not*
> *being loved*

and almost burst into tears, I try hard to fight them back but a few escape. It seems I am so often fighting against my tears. The train passes through torrential rain, and we arrive at Schriever.

I'm the only one getting off. There is no station here, just a pre-fab structure that houses an office and bathroom for the BNSF Railway, Gulf Division. I step out of the train directly onto broken concrete, no platform, circle the pre-fab unit and sit down to smoke a cigarette and call a taxi. There is a long freight train sitting on a pair of tracks, and several houses beyond. It seems this station is only accessible via a small service road, and its real use is for the freight trains, not passenger service. I can hear thunder, and the sky is black and blue, severed by rain clouds. One of the men working here steps out of the office and walks to his truck. I take some comfort in knowing that if the storm comes I can take shelter inside, but soon both men step out, padlock the office door and drive off. I am alone with the highway throb and the buzzing of birds and insects and the thunder in the distance, warm sun on my skin, a heat shimmer on the horizon. I wander around a bit, sleeves rolled up, cigarette burning idly. There are ants everywhere, they swarm in the gravel and broken pavement beneath my feet. It feels good here. I am on my own. I wait two hours for my taxi to arrive. A better writer than I could do this solemnity justice.

My taxi driver has spent time in Maine, working in the paper mill in Augusta or Waterville. He tells me the women in Maine have "cold weather and warm hearts," while the opposite is true in Louisiana. He tells me about the connections between both states, how they have many French, but they drop the X from most French names up there. He spent 8 years in Maine, and I tell him that if it wasn't for the winter I'd be there in a heartbeat. And, thinking about it, I realize I do love it there. I think of a childhood of solitary summers, alone on a lake, indulging in my imagination for 2 months, exploring the water and the wood and my own mind. Hours spent on the water, swimming or floating idly or taking out a canoe and exploring the small island at the center of Coffee Pond. Long walks around the water, creating my own imaginary worlds, filled with heroes and villains, concocting histories and relationships and character arcs. I would lay awake at night in existential terror pondering my own death, wondering what monsters would emerge from the woods outside my window, try to imagine what [lies] beyond the infinite of space. In the morning I would be excited and energized at the prospects new imaginary worlds to invent, new adventures to lead in my mind.

At the Howard Johnson's in Thibadoux the girl at the front desk (her name is ███████) makes a remark about me being from New York. She says she is going to work in Merrimack this summer and as I'm typing this I realize she really said Mamaroneck because she also mentioned Orienta. It seems like things are fated in some sort of way. I kept wanting to go back and talk to her about New York, but aside from asking her for a place to get some food I let my exhaustion take over and laid in bed. Awake now, writing, I feel strange. My body aches, I am physically ill at ease. Uncomfortable. Hopefully, when work starts I will get back into the swing of things.

I sit outside on the bench near the hotel lobby, smoking, my body is more comfortable now. I don't want to be inside. The guests in the next room have been watching tv all day and walking by the ground level rooms near the swimming pool; it seems that most of them are filled with cases of beer.

I sit outside and well up again with tears. This gentle night, this calm place. The enormity of it all, the desperate need to love, to be loved. To not be alone, at this moment, at any moment, to not be crushed by it, or to be crushed but be intertwined with someone else, anything, god, anything at all. Just echoes.

And everything else seems so small in comparison, and I am reaching out, from a distance, from a far away place, from Thibadoux, Louisiana or Casco, Maine or Tucson, Arizona, reaching out through a thousand quiet nights, a cacophonous symphony of buzzing insects, bowed trees swaying, cars like apparitions through dark wooded roads, rain slick blades of grass, an evaporating shadeless summer sun, a heart that bursts.

Before I go to the work site I leave a note for ███████ and tell her to let me know if she wants any suggestions on places to go or things to see. I feel good that I at least made some sort of effort to embrace the cosmic coincidence of our meeting. Whether she ever responds is not important, the fact that I have acknowledged the connectivity of the universe is fulfilling enough. It's how I try to compensate for my natural instincts. As a child [who was] too afraid to climb trees or play sports, I feel I owe it to myself to push against myself in some way [now]. Because naturally, I will just stay in bed all day (the only thing that gets me out is that my thoughts are so viru-lent and toxic that they force me to move so as to somehow alleviate myself of them), I will not leave the house, I will not try anything, I will not in any-way endanger myself [by stepping outside my] afflicted bubble. Sometimes I am better at fighting myself and sometimes I am not, but it is always a struggle, every day, every hour, against my nature and my mind, and as my hope has ebbed away (and I have very little hope or anticipation of happiness or even happiness itself, only sometimes a mild satisfaction at a job somewhat well done, but even that only short lived and not what I think someone would call happiness, no moments of loss of self, no moment when I am not acutely aware of who I am, and what I am doing, and then that information relayed through a toxic filter itself and pumped into my system) it has become harder and harder to do this, or maybe easier, as I am not much more than a shambles, a shit but an honest shit at least.

In Brisbane, [I will be] DJing, 3 days after the end of my trip in Louisiana. Drunk revelers literally make me ill. Watching people stumble and sway, it makes me nauseous. I [will] lay awake in bed in the hotel after the show, after I have left ████████ and he goes after two young dark skinned girls, because I have no interest in sex, not with strangers and fuck not really even with anyone else anymore, sex doesn't matter to me and maybe that's the cause of my state of depression, rather than a symptom; maybe if I cared about fucking people and was able to do that like a normal human being (I used to care a lot) I would feel more normal; thinking about it makes me want to put my head through a window or lop off my sex with a machete. Sometimes I can fuck but only if I've had the right amount of alcohol, and cocaine helps too, but the mere thought of drinking now makes me want to wrap a plastic bag around my head. I still have a beer every now and then, but that's more out of feeling guilted into it by people around me than any-thing else. At parties and when I'm djing if it wasn't for the social guilt I would just sit and sip water silently and write in my head because I do not care about what people have to say. I don't care that you're drunk and think it's an honor to meet me, or want my autograph, because you probably don't even know who I am, and also because I didn't give a shit about my perfor-mance and just wanted to get it over with and get over the body shakes and the cold twisting of my insides and all the anxiety. Fuck I am broken, so beyond broken I wish I had been an abortion. Lying awake in bed I feel an emptiness or a longing for something that can never be had, there is an emp-tiness beyond what I think most people can imagine, and beyond that there is probably a clarity or maybe a resolve that this just isn't worth it anymore, and if I'm not a little phony maybe one day I will reach that.

I take a forty-dollar taxi 15 minutes to the work site on Bon Jovi Boulevard, a loop of replica houses off of Bayou Blue Bypass Road. The house for volunteers is simple, simpler than the other houses in the area, with red concrete floors. The bathrooms have two exhaust fans and I appreciate it, I've found over time I've become more and more self-conscious about taking a shit in a bathroom without one. The porch of the house looks out on the bas-ketball court and playground for the housing development.

The walls of the volunteer house are covered with writing, slogans, drawings, advice and quotes from previous occupants. They tell you where to eat, how good the experience has been. "Go to Boudreaux and Thibodaux's, get 10 pounds of crawfish!" (I go there on my last day working and almost everything on the menu is fried. I want to have gator but not fried, instead I get a mushy sauce with rice and small chunks of gator meat that taste like chicken.) "Go to Bubbas II, get a fried shrimp po' boy!" (I did. It was alright.) "Only the gentle are truly strong – James Dean" Those who have came before are students, youth groups, "ex-fornicators," according to their tags and signatures. I have a room to myself. There are only two other volunteers in the house: ███, a retired electrical engineer in his 60s from Virginia and ████, 17, down for two weeks completing his senior project. ████ is short, shorter than me, with a rotund gut and a noisy way of breathing exclusively through his nose. He smokes more than I do. The day I arrive he drives me to the supermarket, and while listening to Eric Clapton *Unplugged* he tells me that he came down here 8 weeks ago because he felt ashamed about how his country had treated those in the wake of Katrina. He was an electrical engineer for the government, making "bombs that kill babies." He doesn't say it with pride or sadness, but in a cynical, matter-of-fact way. He has intense road rage, violently screaming at other drivers who don't use their turn signals, go to fast, or are too indecisive. He viciously calls one woman a cunt, and ████ tells me after I have returned to New York that he called another man a nigger. This at least confirms that I did correctly overhear him say "whatchu looking to steal nigger" one morning, while I was laying in bed and I assume he was looking out the kitchen window.

Sitting on a porch in front of the volunteer housing domicile, smoking cigarettes under an emancipating sky. Inside, standing, my head resting against a bunk bed, two tears migrate down my cheek. If I am too honest, I am sorry. And if I lie, I am also sorry, because both honesty and falsity seem to bring pain in equal amounts. I just can't seem to get it right. I am so hard on myself.

The workday starts at 7:30. We have coffee and there are two Tupperware containers filled with pre-packaged Danishes, snack cakes, and brownies. There is an AmeriCorps group, they have just arrived from working in Camden, New Jersey. They are young, just out of high school or in the midst of college. They play around with each other, teasing and using pet names and inside jokes that have fermented and grown through their prolonged time together.

Each day my work is different; I spend the first two days hammering nails into the back wall of the house, completely alone and with the sun burning my back. By the end of the first day, after several hours of standing on a ladder and hammering, I begin to say little prayers with each nail I hammer in: "I will be loved," "I am a worthy human being," etc. I still feel empty inside and I still feel apart from most things, and my arm aches and I have to wait a minute before each nail to regain my strength. I get badly sunburnt and make sure to apply sunscreen as often as I can. On the second day, I finish nailing the back wall, this time I get to use a nail gun to speed up the process. As I climb up 15 feet to start working, ▇▇▇▇, an Americorps member who is part of the more long term volunteer staff here comments that he is amazed that no one has lost a limb yet. We hang brackets in the windows and doors, measure bracing and saw pieces of wood to place between wall studs, fill up a cesspool of sewage with dirt and rocks, move lumber, fix other people's mistakes. I make mistakes here and there but I try to work with diligence. I make friends with people, the AmeriCorps kids are nice, but at the same time I feel both very young (physically being small and weak) and old (there is an emptiness inside me that will not go away, and I see futures and happiness and goals and achievements in everyone's lives except for my own). My clothes are ill-fitting, my pants are too baggy, it makes me feel like a 16-year-old. I guess I look like a 16-year-old, but I feel like a 100-year-old. I am always apart, I am never near.

On the last day, we go to a dedication ceremony at another worksite. There is a man who lives near the property that had been cooking free meals for the volunteers during the construction period. He is in his late 50s, with faded tattoos on his arms and a wife with Lou Gehrig's disease. I can't understand a word she says, and the foreman from our work site remarks to him that it's "really fucked up." I guess there's no decorum when describing something like that. He lets one of the kids moving into the house move his car, then talks about how if the car gets messed up he will saw the kid into pieces and feed him to the gators in the swamp, then feed us the gators. He talks about cooking us raccoon, gator, maybe possum but I'm not sure, and says the best way to get an armadillo shell is to just leave the carcass on the ground and let the ants pick the meat, clean it out for you. At the ceremony, a priest blesses the house and each room, sprinkling holy water around. We do the Lord's Prayer, which I remember most of from rehab and AA. Hallowed be thy name... The owners are both crying, and of course, I start tearing up as well, my nose starts running and a cough develops in my throat that I furiously and painfully try to suppress so as not to interrupt the proceedings.

[I think:] What resonates inside you? What does the reverberated echo inside you say? When was the last time you were happy? When was the last time you were excited? When was the last time you looked forward to something? When was the last time you felt okay about feeling okay? When was the last time you enjoyed yourself and felt you deserved it? When was the last time you felt attractive? When was the last time you felt confident? When was the last time you felt good about your creativity?

█████ drives me back to the Schriever station. Waiting for the train to New Orleans, I meet a man who's killed another man. He mentions it in passing; he is worried that he cannot get his haz-mat trucking license in Afghanistan due to a vehicular manslaughter charge. We empty *[out]* the water that has pooled in the chairs by the tracks and sit. He is a rigger, going back to work after a week off in Morgan City, though trucking in Afghanistan is his goal. He says he carries California with him always, and though he was born in Kentucky, all his best friends, "the diamonds," are back home. Money is the only thing in life that matters to him, more than love, for without money, you'll be asking your love to give you cash for the train or for a pack of smokes or for food to eat. He says he can't stand friends who complain about their lovers — they chose them, he says. Either love them wholeheartedly or leave them. *[I agree.]* I tell him it's unfair to be dishonest about that sort of thing, that if you cannot give that love then it's not worth it to keep the person hanging on. He calls me "New York." A small red ant has crawled up my arm and bites me.

I have no hope. Nothing makes me happy. Nothing makes me excited. I hate myself. I feel I am a loser. I am fucking worthless. I have ruined my life. My life is over. This is my fault. I am at the bottom of a deep well, no light can reach me, nobody cares that I am here, this is my fault. When I die there won't be anything left behind of any worth. I am miserable. This is not my fault. This is my fault. I am miserable. I want to die. I want to die. I am shit. I am shit. There is a nothing inside of me. I don't know how to not feel this way anymore. I don't know what to do anymore. I want to die. I want to wrap myself up in a plastic bag I want to be pulverized I want to be ash I want to have never existed I want to have never lived any of this I want to never feel like this again I want to be anyone but me anywhere but here anytime but now. *I am alone I am dead I am lost.* this can't be happening this. can't be happening. this is happening. there isn't a sound in the world that will drown this feeling out. ❖

I am picking you up at the airport,
I want to cry you look so sad,

Language

...AND PLEASE ALWAYS BE AN EXTERNAL EXHIBITIONIST.

They might not care, but the angst gods do.
And always revel in your intelligence, for you can
Put into words what they
Only dream about.
Yes!

– BEN, 1996 – 97

Language is in the body before there are words to express it. More importantly, the pre-linguistic child absorbs the rhythmic and musical elements of the sounds around it. Music creates a world of non-verbal associations that can act as gateways. They may even destabilize the rigid hierarchies of traditional linguistic structures.

It can be identified as a poetic maternal language, the one which is initiated from the body. The semiotic world of sound and rhythm has access to the realm of desires before language becomes a set of solid rules.

I did not "speak" to Ben when he was an infant, but we had our own rich secret language. It was constructed out of sound, mumble, gush, and bubble. It was the most pleasing melody of harmonic compositions—a voice initiated and born from the core of mother, body, and soul.

This was a pure, sensual language that belonged to the two of us. It did not rely on or obey any grammatical structure, intelligence, wisdom, or intellectual message. But it was the sweetest dialog ever, back and forth, my sound followed by an echo resonating from Ben.

It is a universal language, one that joins many mothers across the world, a model that offers boundless openness through the body and the mind. It is essential, forging an even greater connection between mothers and babies. I can always identify a young mother when I see one; I am able to hear that

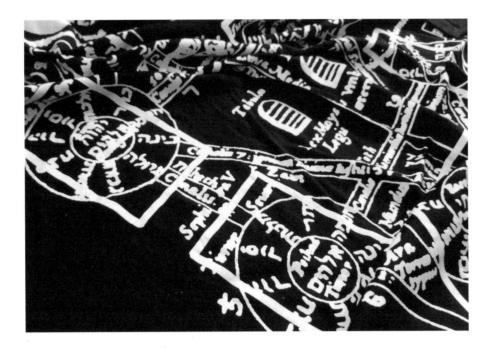

baby language hiding beneath the formal and structured one.

I use different timbres, voicing myself to baby Ben. At times it's the sound of the mellow nostalgic violin. At others, the Allegro of our untuned piano.

When playing silly or reading a story, I become the train, cat, moon, and red flower. My body portrays the image, accompanied by a vocal shift to an exaggerated and somewhat musical form of speech. Always, Ben could decode me. Our rapport is unequaled by any other discourse. Just you and me, a mother speaking to her baby son.[44]

As time went by, I had to surrender to a more complex system of communication, a language that is capable of logic, intricate thought, patterns, and hierarchy. A language that separates the body from the act of speech, a mother from baby, and male from female. My instinctive choice was to speak Hebrew with Ben, because of its strong ties with my own culture and identity. Ben was an early talker and a fast learner and was soon chatting in Hebrew. His first Hebrew word (that came after Ima and Aba) was "OFANOA" or motorcycle. Anything on wheels attracted his attention. The written Hebrew is a phonetic language, but at times does not lend itself to easy pronunciation, especially when it comes to pharyngeal and guttural sounds.[45] The word "ofanoa" was an easy one to pronounce, with no REISH (the sound of R in Hebrew) and no

CHET (the sound is a guttural "hh," as in the "ch" in the name Bach) getting in the way, as they do in so many Hebrew words. In addition, breaking the word up into syllables makes it even more easily legible: *off-no-and a(H)*.

Growing up in Israel in 1950s, I was exposed to many different languages, but Hebrew still defines my identity. It is an intimate territory, a place where I feel the most natural and comfortable. Mastering its grammar and vocabulary enables me to manipulate, mold, form, and shape words in accordance to my own perception, emotion, and culture. This is what in actuality fuses the body and language together.

I am able to detect the root-source of almost any Hebrew word, from biblical to modern times, despite the many stages of its development. It is a true gift that binds us speakers, as individuals, to the community of Israeli culture.

But speaking Hebrew with Ben became complicated, and I got into trouble. Soon I was asked by some family members to stop speaking Hebrew with Ben. It may be that speaking French with him would have been considered superior and more acceptable to them, but not the scary, insignificant Hebrew language.

More importantly, Roger did not understand Hebrew, and Ben began to express frustration in social situations outside his home. So, around his second birthday, I switched from Hebrew to English.

When I got married, my parents gave me a beautiful pearl necklace. Bright white beads interlaced together—a narrative of a family—mine. The existence of one bead depends upon the other, continually holding together past, present, and the fabricated future.

As I gave up speaking Hebrew to Ben, one pearl dropped from this chain. I had to translate myself into a new "me" by digging deeper into an unfamiliar social system, behavior, attitude, and values.[46] I found it harder to communicate in English, and I feared the generational tension that can occur over time when child and parent's first languages differ. It was this way with me and my mother.

Ben was in the fourth grade when his class went on a field trip to visit a real office. They were asked to dress up like the chief executive officer of a company: a white shirt, tie, and a jacket, no sneakers. "The proper traditional outfit," they were told. But I had a different opinion—in Israel, even the Israeli prime minister does not wear a tie, so it should not be required to put one on. In fact, I was quite upset with the request. There was a point I wanted to make about acknowledging different cultural conventions. At the same time, I forgot that I was doing this at Ben's expense; when he got to school without a tie, his teacher reprimanded him. Luckily, the vice principal was very kind and lent him his own. I am forever grateful for the vice principal's attitude.

Looking back, I feel very guilty...

At bedtime, I continued to sing Ben my favorite Hebrew lullaby. It was a bit melancholy, a song by the name "Dugit Nosat."[47]

> A fishing boat is sailing on – her sails are two
> All of her sailors are fast asleep.
> Wind is blowing over the water,
> Silently a child is strolling on the shore.
> He is a small and joyless child,
> Endless water is washing to the far distance…
> If all her sailors don't wake up
> How will the boat reach the shore?

> דּוּגִית נוֹסַעַת, מִפְרָשֶׂיהָ שְׁנַיִם
>
> וּמַלָּחֶיהָ נִרְדְּמוּ כֻּלָּם.
>
> רוּחַ נוֹשֶׁבֶת עַל-פְּנֵי הַמַּיִם,
>
> יֶלֶד פּוֹסֵעַ עַל הַחוֹף דּוּמָם.
>
> יֶלֶד פָּעוּט הוּא וַעֲגוּם-עֵינַיִם.
>
> שׁוֹטְפִים הַמַּיִם לְמֶרְחַק אֵין-סוֹף...
>
> [48] אִם לֹא יֵעוֹרוּ כָּל מַלָּחֶיהָ -אֵיכָה תַּגִּיעַ הַדּוּגִית לַחוֹף ?

I have not been able to sing or listen to music for over a year. When I finished writing about this beautiful lullaby, I needed to sing it out loud. It was the first time after Ben's death that I was able to carry a tune. My mother used to sing it to my sister and me. We loved listening to it. We both had tears in our eyes whenever it was sung.

Endnotes

44. "It's so consistent across mothers." [Dr. Elise Piazza said.] "They all use the same kind of shift to go between those modes." Research has shown that it plays an important role in language learning, engaging infants' emotions and highlighting the structure in language, to help babies decode the puzzle of syllables and sentences. And now, Princeton researchers have identified "a new cue that mothers implicitly use to support babies' language learning," said Elise Piazza, a postdoctoral research associate with the Princeton Neuroscience Institute (PNI). "We found for the first time that mothers shift their vocal timbre. The same mother speaks to a researcher in the Princeton Baby Lab, illustrating the shifts in pitch, cadence and timbre between regular speech and "motherese." "Timbre is best defined as the unique quality of a sound," explained Piazza. "Barry White's silky voice sounds different from Tom Waits' gravelly one — even if they're both singing the same note." She and her colleagues found that the timbre shift was consistent across women who speak 10 languages, including English, and that the differences are strong enough to be reliably picked out by a machine learning algorithm. Their study appears in the journal *Current Biology*. www.cell.com/current-biology/fulltext/S0960-9822(17)31114-4. (This material is excerpted from "Uncovering the sound of 'motherese,' baby talk across languages" by Liz Fuller-Wright from the Princeton University's news site. October 12, 2017.)

45. The sound ר (R) is a semi-guttural. Gutteral sounds are so-called because they are pronounced deep in the throat.

46. "One of the most important functions of language is its role in the construction of reality. Language is not simply a tool for communication, it is also a guide to what [Edward] Sapir terms social reality. Language has a semantic system, or a meaning potential which enables the transmission of cultural values (Halliday 1978: 109). Therefore, while the child is learning language, other significant learning is taking place through the medium of language. The child is simultaneously learning the meanings associated with the culture, realized linguistically by the lexico-grammatical system of the language (Halliday 1978: 23)." (From: Linda Thompson, "Learning Language: Learning Culture in Singapore." *Language, Education and Discourse: Functional Approaches,* ed. by Joseph A. Foley. Continuum, 2004).

47. A *dugit* in Hebrew is a small fishing boat. *Nosat* means travelling.

48. "Dogit Nosat" is a children's poem written in 1943 by Natan Yonatan. The lyrics were composed by Lew Aleksandrowicz Szwarc.

"I am afraid of what is going to happen next, in the long run.
I am afraid of being a marginal character. I am afraid of
being forgotten of losing my way, of failing my potential…"

– BEN, FROM A FREE WRITING EXERCISE, 18 YEARS OLD

Liminal, marginal, and outsider

Each year, the Alexander lectureship invites a distinguished scholar to the University of Toronto to give a series of public lectures. In 1977, Carolyn Heilbronn was invited. Heilbronn is an honored scholar, the first woman to receive tenure in the English department at Columbia University. She spoke about liminality: women's close connection to changing territories—finding themselves in between varying cultural claims, languages and realities.

The word "limen" means threshold. To be in a state of liminality is to be poised upon uncertain ground, on the brink of leaving one condition or country or self to enter upon another. But the most salient sign of liminality is its unsteadiness, its lack of clarity about exactly where one belongs and what one should be doing or wants to be doing.

For Heilbron, liminality is a permanent state, not a transitional phase, as is generally assumed in the field of anthropology.

I could not imagine a better description of my own feelings about my new position in the world. Liminality as a space and state has taken over my life; it has become my new home, a lasting dwelling, which is feeble and weak, located at the edge of society, inferior and marginalized. This is the result of speaking a language not my own, living a culture which is not mine, and losing a son—after which, there are no words that would lift me out of the cocoon in which I now find myself. And yet, Ben, from a young age, is able to convey a similar feeling:

I really don't know. I am terrible at first impressions, I usually make a jackass out of myself... usually, I am not the first person people want to talk to, and if they don't want to talk to me then there is no use in me trying to engage them. Sometimes my humor will disarm people and make it easier to talk to people but sometimes it just weirds people out. I guess I would enjoy talking to an intelligent, bohemian person, but it seems like every person I know like this is so cocky and self-centered that they utterly enjoy force-feeding themselves their own ego.

– AGE 15–16

———————

"You remember me?" he asks, but I don't, and I tell him so. I can't help but stare at his mouth, which is opening and closing like a suffocating fish. Right away I want to free myself from the conversation, but I've never been good at that sort of thing. I can feel myself becoming trapped by his earnestness, caught between a seemingly benign intent and the growing discomfort it's causing me. I usually lack the selfishness to get out of these situations, which is a terrible weakness that leads to a lot of profoundly awkward interactions with the disenfranchised and odd: Autistics, weirdos, sad, wet drunks, people reaching out in various states of desperation and aloneness. I've often seen friends end these sorts of interactions with insults so poorly veiled as to prove the social ineptness of those they're insulting (any normal person would have picked up on the arrogant disregard with which they'd been confronted). Weakness though it may be, I don't have the heart to do it myself. To be honest, these sorts of misfits are the ones I seek out most in social situations. They're the ones around whom I don't have to engage in any pantomime of normalcy. There's something comforting about those who can't even pretend to be okay anymore.

– AGE 17

———————

I am 30 and I still feel as alienated and alone as I did when I was 27 or 17 or 13. Nothing has changed. I am still the same person.

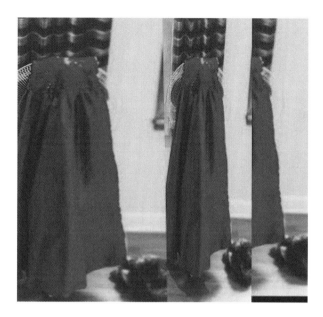

Several years ago, I took a course about women poetry. In my final essay, I discussed poetry written by women living in between cultures. 15 years later I am realizing how it is still relevant for today's world.

If prose seeks accuracy and words that verify, poetry is determined by its sound, tempo, weight and linguistic images. I do not mean to imply that prose is not capable of the same—but it is nowhere near so compact and condensed. My essay concentrates on three poets, women who have experienced an intercultural encounter. This is sometimes also called the "Twilight Zone," a space that exists more than anything else, in a constant jolt between the two categories, trying to mediate between them. I chose three poets:

First is **Gloria Anzaldúa**, who defined herself as a Chicana (American of Mexican descent), and her famous poem "To Live in the Borderlands," has a title used as a metaphor, a phrase that has meaning beyond its tangible meaning. The word "border" expresses the same line of separation, the one that must be clear and precise. But here in this poem, it is an area where tireless vengeance and confusion are held together.

Esther Shkalim is an Israeli poet. In her autobiographical work *Sharkia* ("Fierce Eastern Wind"), she examines femininity, looking at its incarnations and its existence between two different cultural worlds of female lineage: Grandmother, mother, and granddaughter. The grandmother and mother

devote themselves to raising children and family. The granddaughter, a poet, has already been exposed to modern culture and has to redefine herself in a new context. Her grandmother who lived in Iran and raised 15 children knew her place, in contrast to her granddaughter, who is struggling between her own western lifestyle and her kinswomen of origin in the east. She still "hears" the Sharkia winds as a symbol to her struggle. She remains confused. Shkalim ends her book: "What will I do, Mom?"

The third poet, **Tanaya Hdar**, was born in 1947 in a DP[49] camp in Germany to Holocaust survivor parents. Her poem called "Ruth, mainly concerns the realm of the encounter between *Eretz Israel* and the Diaspora, paying attention to the sequence of generations. The biblical Ruth who has crossed borders, religion, and languages has experienced personal suffering for a national mission, as a symbol for all of us who immigrate. The poem begins with Ruth's national destiny, and goes on to talk about the private pain of a widow who has abandoned her homeland and moved to a new country. The poet uses few and very short sentences, conveying to the reader an experience of immigration, death, departure, and adaptation to a new culture.

I was asked as part of my assignment to add a personal poem depicting similar themes. I am not a poet and never wrote one for class. This request thrust me into a emotionally confused state. I lacked confidence. In any event, this is what I wrote privately:

Art by Chagit Deitz

Early this morning, as I glance casually at my mirror
I do not see the queen of England.
Only my five mothers, from five continents,
speaking fluently five languages.
Early this morning,
I do not see the queen of England.
But a reflection of my grandmother,
Drinking her morning coffee
in Vienna.
My mother with her, allowed a small sip.
The mirror was a gift given to my mother,
who moved to Prague—where a medley of languages
have been knitted together.
One knitting needle grows into a guarding tower,
a barbed wired enclosing a death camp.
It was necessary to become careful in the German language.
Now she cradles her babies—in Hebrew, one of them will be nursing in English.

Endnote

49. DP – Displaced persons

There is another home

While I dwell in liminality, there is another home, far away in a small neighborhood on the outskirts of Tel-Aviv: my parents' home, the house where my sister and I grew up. They came to Israel from Europe after World War II. Heinz Angel from Berlin and Eva Goldstein from Slovakia became Dan and Chava Malachi.

After getting reparations from the German government, they bought their first home in a place called Tzahala, a small neighborhood built in the 1950s to house high-ranking officers from the Israeli army and their families. I have no idea what exactly motivated them to choose this location, in such an unfamiliar terrain for them. My only assumption is that they wanted to live in a "good area," as my mother would say. My parents were Holocaust survivors, a badge that no one wished to wear or identify with. Their neighbors represented the "New Israeli," a status that everyone aspired to: liberated from the dark cloud of the *"Shoah"* (Holocaust) and unencumbered by the *"Gola"*—the exile of the wandering Jew.

"Hareut" (friendship, brotherhood) is a Hebrew poem by Haim Gouri written one year after the start of Israel's War of Independence, illustrating the social ideal and spirit of the new country. It describes a love of country sanctified with blood—and remembers the "elegant and handsome" Israeli soldiers who are no longer among us.

The Brotherhood

The eve of autumn falls upon the Negev
And ignites the stars oh so silently
As the wind blows over the threshold
Clouds walk upon the road.

For a year we've barely felt
How the times have passed in our fields
Been a year and so few we are now
For many are no longer among us.

But we shall remember them all
Those with the forelock and the handsomeness
For a brotherhood such as this would never
Let our hearts forget
A love sacred in blood
You shall bloom once again amongst us.

We've carried you with no words, brotherhood
[You were] Gray, stubborn and silent
From the great nights of terror
You remained bright and alight.

As your boys, brotherhood, all of us
Shall again in your name, smile and march on
For brothers that fell upon their sword
Left behind your life for remembrance.

My parents were not a part of this social scene; they maintained their connections with dead relatives, faraway places and cultures. Theirs was a home filled with sadness and never-ending grief. They were very intelligent people. My mother spoke six languages and had an enormous intellectual curiosity. They were fluent in Hebrew (though it did take them some years to learn it) but preferred German. They subscribed to German magazines such as Stern, my father drove a German car, and most of the books in the house were in German, Hungarian and Czech. To this day I wonder of their preference for everything German, in spite of their ruthless journey during the war. They lost most of their family; my mother survived Auschwitz and a labor camp in Germany by working for the aircraft manufacturing corporation Messerschmitt. She outlived the Death March, and yet they were unable to unpeel the scab, expose the wound, let it heal by the fresh air or just a kiss.

My mother's family lived in the same town for over 150 years. When she would speak of them, she would become a little girl again, gasping for air and unable to stop crying. Later on, after losing Ben, I was able to recognize that same little girl in myself, the same cry, the endless sobbing of a broken heart.

I aspired to live outside and beyond my parents' home, where there was so much pain. I wanted to be like everybody else. I was living a double life: one inside my home and another outside, for the neighborhood milieu to see. Perhaps I was not unlike Ben, who lived within himself and the image he worked so hard to project.

> I have always felt like I was on the outside looking in. This is
> exemplified by my upbringing. I was born in Westchester but went
> to High School in Manhattan, initially at ▮▮▮▮▮▮▮ School. There I
> always had a slight sense of being an outsider. I was neither a city
> kid nor a suburban kid. This feeling would carry over to times spent
> with my suburban friend as well. And it would continue to follow me
> throughout my life, a [persistent] feeling that I never quite belonged.

Poprad

When Ben was about 12, we took him to visit Poprad, the town in Slovakia that had been my mother's family's home before the war. We traveled by bus from Vienna to Bratislava (the capital of Slovakia), and then took an old Russian train to Poprad. When we got out of the train, we found ourselves in an old run-down building. We felt uneasy, as we were surrounded by some kids, mostly Romanies, who drew near us, staring at "the Americans" and requesting—almost pleading for—some coins. We were eager for our taxi to arrive and take us to the hotel.

Photo of my great-grandfather, Shimon Goldstein his wife and their children.

Poprad is in the north of Slovakia, at the foot of the Tatra mountains. Today it is a well-known resort town. It is also the starting point of the Tatra Electric Railway (known in Slovak as Tatranská elektrická železnica), a set of special narrow-gauge trains (trams) connecting the resorts in the High Tatras with each other and with Poprad.

My mother used to tell us so many stories about her hometown, usually in a graphic manner that depicted the natural landscape, the architecture of the homes and buildings, as well as the local residents "and their standing in the community." Despite her claims of egalitarianism, she was a bit of a snob.

She did not have many old photos to share with us, but there was no need for such objects, as her ability as a storyteller was well known. I remember one time, when she gathered all the kids around her and told them that bears are born from eggs. The adults present were upset, but this was so typical

My grandmother, Henrietta (center), my mother (second from left), and her siblings.

of her, simply her way. At times she may have embellished the narrative, but truth be told, it worked. We were a rapt audience.

Photo of my grandparents, Izidor and Henrietta and my mother, in Poprad before the war

My recollection of the visit has very little to do with the outside terrain and views and more to do with our interface, the common boundary enabling the inner landscape to communicate with the outside panorama. We were revealed and exposed in new ways, just by being in that setting, with all its history.

We were able to easily find the house belonging to my great grandfather William Krieger, where my grandmother Henrietta was born in 1895. Later on, as family legend goes, she escaped through the window of that house in order to marry my grandfather, Isidor Goldstein.

At the beginning of the 20th century, the Jewish community grew, and most of Poprad's Jews made their living from

My great grandfather's wine store on the left, my great aunt and my mother on the right.

trades and crafts. They owned about 40 businesses, 13 workshops, and some enterprises, among them the lumberyard owned by Heinrich Engländer that employed about 150 workers; a factory for strong liquors "Kleinberger & Sons"; William Krieger's factory for yeast and starch; and three other small enterprises. Some of Poprad's Jews were professionals: two out of the four doctors in town; three of the four lawyers; a pharmacist; a midwife and a few engineers and clerks. Dr. Max Singer served as the district doctor.

The Krieger family, my mother's family, was a prominent family in Poprad. William Krieger, my great grandfather, was the owner of the yeast and starch company. My mother's uncle was the lawyer, and her favorite aunt Klara Goldstein, born in 1904, was the pharmacist ("chemist"). William Krieger, my great grandfather, was not only a businessman who owned the yeast and starch company. According to several records, he was also one of the two co-founders of the first railway connecting Poprad and Starý Smokovec, which was built in 1906–07, also known as the "Tatra Trolley"—the predecessor of the modern Tatra Electric Railway. To carry this ambitious plan out, William Krieger had rented a hydropower plant to provide sufficient electrical power for the train.

My mother's family did not follow a traditional Jewish lifestyle. The three sisters, Eva, Agi, and Susanka, along with their brother younger Michael,

My great grandfather and my great aunts.

attended secular schools. I doubt that any of them attended services at any of the local synagogues, though it's possible that my great grandfather William Krieger did.

Ben and Roger and I devoured the local foods. I was familiar with some of the Slovak dishes: potato pancakes and dumplings, cheese fried in breadcrumbs, Wiener schnitzel, and cabbage. These dishes represent the true mixture of the three cultures that had met here over the centuries: German, Hungarian and Austrian. Beer flowed like water, a must for every meal and in between, always served in a large glass.

We were able to locate the liquor store owned before the war by grandpa Simon Goldstein, of course, it was now selling different merchandise and no longer featured the same signboard: Goldstein Wine and Liquor.

When looking for the Jewish cemetery, in the hopes of finding William Krieger's grave, who had died before World War II, we came across a ruined and even frightening site.

Good networking is always essential. Due to some good connections that Roger had established sometime prior with a Slovak lawyer, we were welcomed into the municipality building, where we asked to see any records pertaining to the Goldstein and Krieger families. One of the clerks went down to the basement of the building where the local town's archive is kept and quickly returned with a very large and heavy black binder. It held the records of birth, dwelling, death, and also the relatives of each person born in this area going as far back as the mid-1800s and up to World War II.

We were able to find most of my mother's family's records, handwritten in black ink with a fountain pen. There it was in black and white: proof of my heritage and identity. A long list of names, members of my family, were included and recognized. I had to hold back tears, as a bewildered look took over Ben's face. It was his first actual glimpse into his tangible heritage and roots all encased in a "black box"...

Most of my relatives were murdered during the Holocaust, as the deportation of Jews from Slovakia started on March 25, 1942, from Poprad railway station. The tragic or dramatic irony is embedded in facts of history itself. This train station is also the southern terminus of the metre gauge, Tatra Electric Railway, the one that was built under the initiative and with the financial support of my great grandfather.

The family trip was of great significance to us all. It was a walking tour amidst pleasure, curiosity, and a great tragedy.

My great grandfather Simon Goldstein.

Elie Wiesel, the Nobel laureate, once said that "the online database of the Shoah Victims' names creates a link not only with the dead but also among the living within the Jewish people. It strengthens the connections between families, between cities, between communities. Furthermore, it brings a heightened awareness and a deepened sense of remembrance."[50] That database listed most of the victims' names on my mother's side of the family. Some of the information was brief, indicating only name, date of birth, and place of residence during the war. Some others contained additional details:

Izidor Goldstein, murdered

Michael Nikol Goldstein, date of birth 1928, murdered

Shimon Goldstein, murdered

Elizabeta Goldstein, date of birth 1906, murdered

Regina Goldstein, date of birth 1895, murdered

Aetel Goldstein, date of birth 1873, murdered

Teodor Goldstein, murdered

Herzi Goldstein, murdered

Medi Goldstein, murdered

Klara Goldstein, date of birth January 21, 1904. Place of birth: Mnsisek. Profession: Chemist. Place during the war: Poprad District. Origin of deportation: Poprad. Destination of Deportation: Auschwitz, Poland. Details of transport: Transport from Poprad to Auschwitz on April 3, 1942. Prisoner number in Transport: 739

Henrietta Goldstein, date of birth 1895, murdered

Imrich Krieger, date of birth 1901. Imerich Krieger was born in Poprad. He was an uradnik. Prior to WWII he lived in Zvolen, during the war he was in Kremnicka. He was murdered and buried in a mass graves in Kremnica, 05/11/1944 – 09/02/1945

Ferdinand Krieger, date of birth 1922, murdered

Margita Krieger, date of birth 1920, murdered

Filip Krieger, date of birth 1900, murdered. Deported with Transport from Poprad, Spis, Slovakia, Czechoslovakia to Izbica, Krasnystaw, Lublin, Poland on 30/05/1942

Carlota Krieger, date of birth 1912, murdered

Zoltan Krieger, date of birth 1912, murdered

Ludwig Krieger, date of birth 1989, murdered

Miska Krieger, date of birth 1888, murdered

Jana Krieger, date of birth 1911, murdered

As we stood by my great grandfather's home in Poprad, a large and handsome house made out of stucco, painted in heather green, we once again were witnessing a marginal, liminal and outsider dwelling; we were far from heaven.

Endnote

50.   Quote source: www.yadvashem.org/archive/hall-of-names/database.html

"Famine" by Edward Delaney

Generational trauma

And once again a woman's hand appears, fully
extended and outstretched. A few blue pigmented numbers are etched
on her arm. Creases of older skin make it hard to decipher some of the
numbers. The hand is, here again, not to lend support but to transmit
trauma, terror, and anxiety across generations.

What does the human being consist of, if not a natural palimpsest?[51] We are
many layers of visual images, memories, ideas, and sensations. Each layer
of our being is buried beneath previous ones, but nothing is really termi-
nated or abolished. We always stay put and remain slaves to our elemental
private and collective memories of previous lives. All facets of life lay naked
and exposed.

My mother and father were the "first generation," the survivors, pos-
sessed by the demons of their past trauma. I am endowed with the unfortu-
nate title of "second generation," a memorial candle for what once was, tasked
with the impossible mission of giving meaning to my parents' survival.

Many years ago, I come home early from school. I hear my mother. She
is sitting in the kitchen by herself all alone, reading out loud from a book written in Hungarian. She is losing her mind, I fear. Looking back, I should have
understood her frail mental state long before this episode. She was always
walking the fine line between sanity and insanity. But what child wants to
accept a broken parent, broken childhood or broken self?

As I listened to my mother's stories of her past life, a realization began
to form: Our mother-daughter relationship is built upon disaster and heart-
break. Seeds of trauma were planted and nourished, breeding branches of anxiety, fear of separation, and depression.

Alongside my mother's history is also my father's, Ben's grandfather's
difficult life story. Heinz Engel, who would later in life become Dan Malachi,
was a quiet man who never shared with us the details of his past. But his
silence could not erase his painful journey into adulthood.

My father was the quiet one. There was not much room for his voice. My mother was the storm and the rain. I can see him very clearly sitting in his armchair with the tall back and yellowish corduroy upholstery entwined with faded brown colors. It was a simple Danish chair from 1960 that echoed style, comfort, and affordable prices. This was my father's domain, where he would hide behind the evening newspaper. On cold nights he would smoke a cigar or light his pipe. Not speaking about his past.

What I know about his life, I learned from my mother, family, and my father's friends: He was born and raised in Berlin. By November 1940, the city had become truly hostile to Jews. At 15 years old, in order to save his life, my father was sent to what was then Palestine. His journey was aided by an organization called Youth Aliyah,[52] which, among other things, operated ships carrying refugees from European ports to Palestine. Upon their arrival in the port of Haifa, the passengers of the dilapidated old vessel were denied entry into the country. The British authorities, which ruled the land at the time, decided to deport these refugees from Nazi-occupied Europe to Mauritius, a British colony. Having escaped a burning Europe, the Promised Land remained at arm's length, the dream of permanency fast disappearing.

The SS Patria had over 1,800 Jewish refugees on board when she was the victim of a bomb plot.

As they and other Jewish refugees from Europe were waiting that morning in the port of Haifa to be transferred onto a French-built ocean liner, the 11,885-ton *SS Patria*, tragic events were about to unfold.

To prevent the shameless deportation of the Jewish refugees, the Haganah resistance organization, together with other paramilitary groups that operated in the land at the time, decided to place a small explosive device on the ship to destroy its motors and keep the ship in port. A miscalculation in the placement of the bomb caused a large explosion that blew the steel frame off of one side of the ship, causing it to sink in less than 16 minutes. British and Arab boats were able to rescue most of the passengers, but about 267 were killed. My father was able to swim to shore.

On November 25, 1940, a 15-year-old boy was pushing his body beyond limits, coming and going, fighting against the waves, *life upon these shores*.[53]

> *Where is He who brought them through the sea with the shepherds of His flock?*
> *Where is the One who set His Holy Spirit among them, who sent His glorious*
> *arm to lead them by the right hand of Moses, who divided the waters before*
> *them to gain for Himself everlasting renown, who led them through the depths*
> *like a horse in the wilderness, so that they did not stumble?*
> ISAIAH 63:11–13, BEREAN STUDY BIBLE

As my father stepped foot onto the terra firma of a new world, embracing new possibilities and challenges, he was unaware of the awful events that were about to unfold west of him in Berlin, the place he used to call home. Antoine (Tony) and Oscar Engel, his parents, his older brother Leo, and his young brother Peter, had remained in Berlin during the war. Tony Engel was born in 1898; Oscar Engel was born in 1893; Peter Engel, my uncle, was born in 1938.

On August 15, 1942 all of them were deported in Transport 18, Train Da 401, from Berlin to Riga, Vidzeme, Latvia, where they were murdered. Leo was taken to Auschwitz where he remained till the camp's liberation. Later, he would emigrate to Israel, and reunite with his brother—my father.

My grandmother was 48 years old, Oscar my grandfather was 53 years old, and Peter my uncle, a child of four years old.

My father has persisted in his silence.

Ben entered into this world, and a new title was born: "third-generation."

All the memories belonging to those who did not, in fact, live the trauma themselves grow out of oral stories, photos, poetry, literature, music, and the proximity to pain. At the same time, they leave boundless space for imagery

and creativity. This generation is tormented by both true and fictional narratives, shaped inside their imaginary and actual universe.

Ben was in his early 20s when we visited my cousin and her family in Prague. Without hesitation, we agreed to visit Terezin, once a military fortress, later converted into a concentration camp by the Nazis during World War II. It was very a cold day with below-freezing temperatures. Ben was moving very slowly, unusual for a fast walker like him, and I wondered if he was ok, since he had been suffering from a bad cold. I asked him if he felt ill. "No Mom, it is not my cold, it is this place. I don't think that I can take it, I feel like fainting." I can still see him even now, wearing his heavy orange winter coat, blue heritage Nordic hat and mittens, storm chasers winter boots, all the way from LL Bean in Freeport, Maine, and the pale, colorless white skin of his face, as we walked the grounds of Terezin.

The Holocaust struck a particularly strong chord with Ben. There were times when he would fool around, telling dark jokes to his cousin, announcing that his marriage will actually take place in Auschwitz. Ben would say that only third-generation relatives will be invited. We totally got it and even giggled, shaking away the "Shoah" heavy burden resting upon our shoulders.

My mother and father would whisper to each other in German. I didn't understand the words, but the same melancholy tune was always present.

My imagination would travel into secret lives of past pain, assisted by the shame I felt simply for existing.

My mother had a collection of books devoted to the Holocaust. From a young age, I would look inside them, mainly glancing at the photographs attached to the text. *Scourge of the Swastika* by Lord Russell of Liverpool was one of those treasured books. It carried me through the perplexing and almost pleasurable journey of exploring lives that did not belong to me; painful as it was, I longed to be closer to their experience. I was so intimate with my mother's suffering, and yet, it was always held just slightly out of reach, an untraversable distance. The many black and white photos, a silent testimony of true events from concentration camps, did not require any translation alongside the printed words. All the horror was right there, laid out before my very eyes. They helped to bridge the gap.

I couldn't stop staring at the pages of the book, as if by studying each one of them, I could decipher some hidden moral logic for the evil that actually took place. I received a transfusion from my optic nerve into my own veins; it did not feel like a second-hand memory, but was instead the start of a solitary journey with remembrances that captivated all of my being.

I am now looking inside the book, seeing an old black and white photo. It captures a group of naked women arriving into camp, running naked one after the other, lining up to be examined by the camp doctor. They are exposed to the cold air. Any German soldier who so wishes is able to stare at their bare body and soul.

Now I see my mother's body, the one which gave birth to me; and my own, which gave birth to Ben. Three generations of memory transmission, shared pain and embodiment: We are bound.

Endnotes

51. A palimpsest *(/pæl´•ımp•sɛst/)* is a manuscript page, either from a scroll or a book, from which the text has been scraped or washed off so that the page can be reused for another document. en.wikipedia.org/wiki/Palimpsest.

52. Youth Aliyah means Youth Immigration. This is an organization established by the determination and passion of a woman called Recha Freier. In the course of the harrowing years that followed, Youth Aliyah saved the lives of thousands of Jewish children by bringing them to Palestine and Great Britain.

53. Lifted from "Middle Passage" by Robert Hayden.

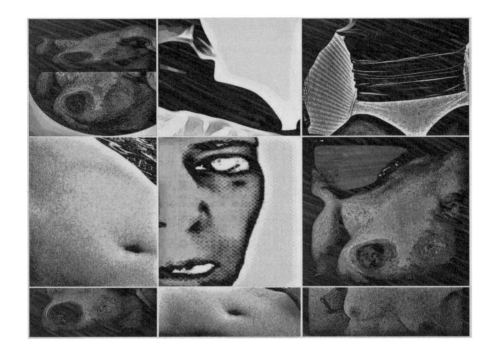

Art by Chagit Deitz

Who could understand what we are going through

Trauma, anxiety, stress, shame, and depression all found favorable stomping grounds within my parents' home. The same was also true of my own home later in life; these mental and physical states transferred themselves biologically, beyond cataclysmic events, from one generation to the next.

This phenomenon has a name: epigenetics.[54] It is the study of gene expression can be altered (and inherited) without being spelled out or "coded" in our DNA; in this way, life experiences can be passed down.

Professor Rachel Yehuda is a researcher in the field of epigenetics who specializes in how traumatic events suffered by an individual might impact the lives of their future children and their offspring. According to Dr. Yehuda, descendants of Holocaust survivors have different stress hormone profiles, ones which compromise their ability to bounce back from trauma[55] and which predispose them to anxiety disorders.

Multigenerational trauma researchers study many different collective and personal devastating events, as well as the strong linkage between trauma and addiction. For example, in a personal interview, Dr. Gabor Mate[56] spoke of his own journey moving through childhood trauma and his battle with addiction later in life. Maia Szalavitz also sets aside all arrogance and shame, writing about her personal connection to the Holocaust (as third-generation) and her own addiction to drugs.[57]

Trauma and addiction reside in the same dwelling, evident in the complex realm of isolation, seclusion, stigma, and shame. Both are the building blocks of a new home; a hiding place out of sight, where the pain one endures remains unspoken.

Who would understand what we are going through?

How do those suffering from addiction and trauma convey their pain to others? The world between worlds into which they travel and fall is the world of a leper. Are we being punished?

> "When a person has the mark of the defiling disease, his clothing must have a tear in it, he must go without a haircut, and he must cover his head down to his lips. 'Unclean! Unclean!' he must call out. As long as he has the mark, he shall remain unclean. Since he is unclean, he must remain alone, and his place shall be outside the camp."
>
> LEVITICUS 13:45–46, BEREAN STUDY BIBLE

How can a mother who has lost a child communicate her grief to others?

When I am asked about Ben's death, I always fear silence or an uncomfortable bodily response headed my way. Those flinches resonate, heighten my pain.

My family and my close friends were very supportive, especially those who knew Ben. But after a loss of that magnitude, in some sense, one is always apart.

What are they thinking? I wonder as insecurity settles within me: Do they think my son was filth? A junkie? That he had weak character? Do they judge me and Roger, wondering why didn't we as parents face up to the problem?

I remain silent.

"Call me sometime," I hear as I walk away defeated, mumbling to myself, *You might get a call of your own one day*. It can happen to anyone.

Historian Raul Heilberg[58] proposes that a new framework must be adopted, which he dubs the "language of trauma." The traditional "practice of [treating] trauma" must depart from the conventional historical archive and methodologies. It must defer to art (e.g. poetry, storytelling, films, music, dance, etc.)

> Trauma escapes language, as the common language in most cases is detached from the experience itself; thus, any attempt to put into words the traumatic experience would depend upon inflated and banal clichés. It seems to me that our society chooses to remove or forget the notion of trauma and at the same time would prefer to ignore the bearer of such experience.[59]

The act of translating anguish into art serves as a therapeutic and healing journey, as well as an emotional cannonball; it connects the observer to the tormented life stories of real people.

Artwork in all forms brings home a dart directed at the heart. A visceral jab at the nervous system, but necessary for sympathy, knowledge, awareness, and support, erasing shame and stigma.

Most of us associate trauma with harrowing events, however, I would like to look into traumatic events within the scope of a normal life as well. For some, trauma could be falling from a bicycle, or a minor car accident, losing a pet, or similar. All people do not cope with stress with the same emotional response. For Ben, just driving from our home to Brooklyn caused tremendous stress and anxiety; he often needed to stop driving as he would break into a cold sweat and need to vomit. I can still remember when I was seven years old, my cat died and my parents kept it a secret for some time. When I found out, the pain was unbearable; I can still feel it, even now.

Virginia Woolf, with regard to the sexual abuse that she suffered by her half-brother Gerald Duckworth, stated, "Nothing has really happened until it has been described," highlighting the connection between the act of trauma itself and the ways in which it is revealed and exposed. [60] Expression is an act that seeks healing, and at the same time, conveys the unimaginable to others. Woolf chose to record her trauma through the art of writing literature. What she was unable to speak about came to life through her stories. She did not narrow her troubles only to her sexual abuse at home but was also concerned with many other traumatic events throughout her lifetime. Her book *To the Lighthouse* was a mournful and barren insight into the death of her parents; *The Waves* is a "novel-poem" about six friends wrestling with the death of a beloved friend. Her book *Jacob's Room* was inspired by the death of her beloved brother Toby, who tragically died at the age of 25. In fact, all of Virginia Woolf's writing focused on trauma, and she was able to get away from the ordinary language used to discuss it, by departing from archives or historical facts, and instead transforming it into art. She had creative license, and that made all the difference.

Rick Bartow, a Native American artist, told *Cultural Survival Magazine* in 2007 that: "I had buried a lot of monsters with alcoholism and drug abuse, and when they started getting out of the box, I lost the lid and couldn't put it back." As a way of coping and communicating his trauma to others, he turned to art.

Times Insider delivers behind-the-scenes insights into how news, features, and opinion come together at *The New York Times*. In December, 2018, *Times* journalists were searching for a different method to portray the opioid crisis.[61]

The resulting article was called "'You Can Make It Out': Readers Share Stories of Opioid Addiction and Survival" and was turned into "A Visual Journey Through Addiction."[62] Journalists Shreeya Sinha and Jennifer Harlan interviewed dozens of people who have used heroin about their personal experiences. Using qualitative research methods, they identified seven categories—or as they called it, the "seven-stages explainer: gateway, tolerance, withdrawal, addiction. treatment, relapse, and recovery." After completing this process, Meghan Louttit (the *Times* editor who organized the package) and the art director Rumsey Taylor read the interviews and searched for an artistic approach drawing on the interviewees' subjective experiences. Louttit and Leslie Davis, the *Times* video journalist, together with software artist Zach Lieberman[63] came up with an idea: A dancer, Bailey Anglin, gave his own somatic interpretation of the words used by the interviewee. Later, Z. Lieberman would manipulate the video recording, adding an atmospheric state of ambiance to convey the warm thrill of an initial high. They layered the video with spiky, discordant static to get across the pain of withdrawal.

This methodology brings up old memories.

Ben is 10 years old; he is in fourth grade. His teacher is a smart woman; to my mind, she is somewhat intense, pushing for the academic and lacking, at times, the tender touch much needed by young pupils.

One of the most important assignments requested by her was to write a personal journal, to be submitted to her once or twice a week. I had mixed feelings about requiring 10-year-olds to share their private thoughts and feelings for a grade. I believe a personal journal should at most times stay private, not subject to academic criteria.

If there is one good thing about journal writing, it is the clearing of the mental chaos one endures. Without a doubt, this was a complex task for many of Ben's schoolmates. Ben was fortunate, as he loved to write. He also had an early ability to recognize his own emotions as well as others'. Ben's journal notebook from fourth grade is still here, carefully stowed on a shelf in my own library. An entry from January 1993 brings up a book much loved by him called *Maus*.

Maus is a graphic novel by Art Spiegelman, an American cartoonist and the son of a Holocaust survivor. It depicts an interview with his father about his life as a Polish Jew during the second world war. Beautiful sketches along with just a few words transmit the history of tragic past events, the fragile existence of the present, and the complicated relationship between a survivor father and his son.

01/01/93

Yesterday I stayed up until 12:00 (for obvious reason). I was so tired I got up at 10:30 this morning.

Yesterday I was reading a magazine about comics (*Wizard*) and it suggested reading section the author wrote about good holiday presents (This was a December issue). Of course, I started reading. The first comic he wrote about was Art Spiegelman's *Maus*. It was the story of his father's life (not a really great life, at that) in Auschwitz. Mr. Spiegelman shows the Jews as mice, the Nazis (actually, all the non-Jewish Germans) as cats, the Americans as dogs, the French as frogs, and the non-kosher people (that doesn't really make sense, but, I couldn't think of anything else, as pigs). Then I suddenly had a brainstorm, a few years ago, I remember my mother reading that book! So, I asked her where it was (she returned home from Israel two days ago (Wednesday). She told me where it was. I went to look, and found it! I started reading little bits of it, and soon I was hooked! The only problem is that it is book two of two, so, I REALLY want to find book one. If you haven't read it. I suggest you do. The book tells how Vladek (Art's father) Spiegelman went through World War II, and how he is after it. It also shows a real-life photo of Vladek. The book is humorous, sad, interesting, everything you want in a book. As I said before, I suggest you try to find a copy of both books.

PS. HAPPY NEW YEAR !!!!!!!!!!!!!!!!!!!!!!!!!!!!!!!!!!!!!!!

– BEN'S 4TH GRADE JOURNAL, AGE 10

01/17/93

Even though I wasn't in school, and was sick, I did my homework (the long math problem was fun and easy).

My current event is about an exhibition in the St. Atien Gallery N.Y.C. about the making of the book *Maus* (Mrs. Crow[64] will know what I'm talking about). I choose that as my current event because I have read the books (which are excellent (see my journal entry about the book for more information). The exhibit is entitled "The Road to *Maus*." I found out about the exhibition when my mom read about it in the Israeli newspaper.

One very interesting thing I found out about Art Spiegelman (the author/illustrator) is that he was one of the illustrators of the sick and funny cards/stickers series "Garbage [Pail] Kids"(you don't want to hear or see anything about/of them).

I was wondering if I could reread one of the books for a non-fiction book. The only problem is that the books are comics.

"NO GOOD" was the teacher's remark: non-fiction comics don't count. Yet in 1992 *Maus* won the Pulitzer Prize. It became the first graphic novel to win a Pulitzer Prize (the Special Award in Letters). The *Wall Street Journal* called it "the most affecting and successful narrative ever done about the Holocaust" and *The New Yorker* declared it "the first masterpiece in comic book history."

Again, my son, you are ahead of the game. I am not sure if your teacher actually grasped the full importance of this book; either way, she did not allow herself to go beyond conventions of the time. It was not the first or last time that you were misunderstood by others, but you managed to accept it gracefully.

The interviewees in the *New York Times* opioid article gave accounts of treatment and relapse, the trauma that was their everyday experience of being addicted. Matt Statman of Michigan described his early highs: "I remember feeling like I was exhaling from holding my breath for my whole life. Just intense relief from suffering." Jasmine Johnson of Pennsylvania said, about withdrawal, "It's like a demon crawling out of you. You'd rather just die and be done with it than go through that."

Testifying. Your journals later on in life were an outlet for you, a practice that allowed you to vent trauma. How much they have meant to me, in your absence, I cannot begin to say. To hear your voice, to be your witness. It is not easy reading about your pain, but at least in this way you are seen, and not silenced.

Endnotes

54. "In its modern sense, epigenetics is the term used to describe inheritance by mechanisms other than through the DNA sequence of genes. It can apply to characteristics passed from a cell to its daughter cells in cell division and to traits of a whole organism. It works through chemical tags added to chromosomes that in effect switch genes on or off." "Epigenetics – It's not just genes that make us" by Dr. Ian Cowell for the British Society for Cell Biology bscb.org/learning-resources/softcell-e-learning/epigenetics-its-not-just-genes-that-make-us/.

55. Taken from "Descendants of Holocaust Survivors Have Altered Stress Hormones" by Tori Rodriguez. *Scientific America*, March 1, 2015. Also noteworthy: From *www.sciencedaily.com* Studies on survivors of traumatic events have suggested that exposure to stress may indeed have lasting effects on subsequent generations.

56. This information was taken from an interview with Dr. Gabor Maté. drgabormate.com/topic/addiction/.

57. Maia Szalavitz in her book *Unbroken Brain: A Revolutionary New Way of Understanding Addiction*.

58. Raul Hilberg, Austrian-born American historian (1926–2007), established the field of Holocaust studies with his comprehensive yet controversial study "The Destruction of the European Jews" (1961). Taken from: *The Generation of Post memory: Writing and Visual Culture After the Holocaust* by Marianne Hirsch (Columbia University Press, 2012).

59. "Trauma escapes language, but so does life." *www.traumatheory.com/trauma-escapes*. Posted by calford@umd.edu on July 12, 2016.

60. "Virginia Woolf and the Language of Trauma" by Loren Kleinman. *Ploughshares*, January 20, 2018. Quote originally from Virginia Woolf by Nigel Nicolson (Lives Series, Weidenfeld & Nicolson, 2000).

61. www.nytimes.com/2018/12/27/us/opioid-addiction-reader-response.html.

62. www.nytimes.com/interactive/2018/us/addiction-heroin-opioids.html.

63. instagram.com/Zach.Lieberman.

64. I think that she was a substitute teacher for a while, as his regular teacher was Mrs. ███████████.

The labyrinth

Photo taken by Ben's very good friend Brigitte after cutting his hair —
a month before his death.

I've spent years suffering from utter anhedonia, wishing I was dead,
consumed by total self-loathing....I've been a liar and a cheat and a
thief, all in service of my addiction... I've ruined relationships with
those I loved, I've destroyed my parents' trust. I've let people down.
I've let myself down.

Now I am walking through a complex maze, making my mind hazy and confused, and challenging within me an internal moral dilemma.

I am attempting to write about Ben's struggle with addiction and depression, less from my perspective or from any other sources, and instead leaning heavily on his short journal written in February and March 2013, along with a heartbreaking letter to us, and some periodic essays that help to unmask his struggle.

Obviously, this journal includes a different kind of writing; it is very personal and expressive, at times confused, and connected to times that were almost impossible to bear.

I can see you casting an agonizing look toward me, you are angry.

Privacy was the most coveted elements of your life.

You guarded your secret with fear, rage, and courage, all at once, as your battle for sobriety took place behind closed doors. Only a few of us had the idea of what is going on and how serious it was.

Gradually, shame took over your life. And I am breaking my promise to you of silence, though not without sorrowful doubts.

The maple chair in Dad's office is still there, witnessing you coming into his room, breaking down after a busy day in the city: group and individual therapy, AA meetings, and also you are attending two different schools, completing a degree in English literature while training to become a substance abuse counselor. Pausing for a short break, you would deposit your tired body and soul into Dad's office, seeking his kindness and a single handmade wooden chair.

The chair is still there, your light OAK jacket hugging the back of it, you are there again and forever, asking Dad to shut the door when speaking about your struggle with addiction.

"There are sores which slowly erode the mind
in solitude like a kind of canker."

– SADEGH HEDAYAT, *THE BLIND OWL*

OUTPUT

a body without motion or presence
my breath hangs frozen in air
grasping for some sort of essence
a structure that was never there

To maintain this moment of purity
It drifts away on the tide
and slips far beyond the horizon
and squeals like the sun as it dies
I'm indebted to you for the feeling

From Ben's journal:

2.1.13

I feel like I have to spend the rest of my life trying to deprogram the
way my parents made me. If only they had raised someone to be
hardworking and diligent. But then again, I used to be hardworking
and diligent about my music, during the times in my life when it
mattered. I just wasn't making good music. Although when I did, I
got recognized. But I do feel unrecognized and like I just can't "make
it." Besides the fact that the stress of it all was literally killing me. I
really feel like that first **Passions** EP was something special. But of
course, I was straddled with a horrible label. Who knows if this
repress is going to happen. I just do not trust ███████. It's too
bad. I really think people need to hear this. My hope is that people
will like the work with ████████. enough that someone will want
to repress the original EP. But who knows? Knowing my luck, the
work with ████████. just won't get the attention it deserves. And
goddamnit it does deserve to be paid attention to. I truly think I'm
making good music now, I know I am, considering I have everyone
from █████ from ██████████ to █████ from ██████████ &
██████████ telling me how good it is and how much they "love" it.
And yet we just can't breakthrough. I guess that's just the way it
is with music. I want recognition. I want to be recognized as the

artist I think I am. I want to be praised and I want to be adored and I want to be paid attention to because there is a small sliver of myself that is talented and unique and it's the only good part of me I have left because the rest is a money-wasting drug addict who is truly truly truly pathetic. I have reached such an epic low. A 30-year-old man … who has wasted about 60,000 dollars on heroin in less than a year and who just cannot get his shit together … Who doesn't even have someone to hold him and rock him to sleep and tell him it's going to be okay and that he does have the strength to beat this. I do have the strength to beat this. I've done this before. Maybe deep down I just don't want to get my act together. Maybe I'm afraid of how much work it will take to keep it up, and how bad I am at keeping it up. I can only do so much; I'm not built to handle too many things. If I could just be sober. I need to be sober. I wish I was sober.

2.5.13

I'm afraid I'm not going to be able to do it. School. I'm down to three stamps, three Adderall, and hopefully tomorrow I get a Xanax prescription. Hopefully, I can make this work. If only I can find the strength to push myself. If I make it through this, I can conquer anything.

2.6.13

Tried to quit today. Fumbled and bought 5 buns. Got Xanax though. Maybe that will help. Have one Adderall. I can do this.

How is it that everyone else is able to make it work? I know people say like, oh everyone is going through what you are going through, but quite honestly, they're not. I don't know anyone who's gone through what I have. Not a single soul. Who the hell else has traveled around the world as a DJ, then quit and spent three years writing a Goth record, and then quit that and started a krautrock band, etc. etc. How many people are unable to hold down a job, a relationship, anything? How many people have had the opportunities that I've squandered? I don't get it. There's really no one who I can sympathize with or who can sympathize with me. I have a headache. I hope this dope I bought is not bad. I just want to have accomplished one good thing, quitting heroin. Then I can move onto the next things. Although it doesn't work like that. It's constant diligence. I should delete my numbers. Three dope dealers! That's pretty good. I can't have a GF while I'm on heroin. I can't really do anything. I need to get off this shit and then move on to the next stage in my life.

I have had it simultaneously easier and harder than everyone. I have money and don't have to work and at the same time, I have no motivation sometimes. I'm lazy. I haven't accomplished what I could have at this point. I just need to try my best and work my hardest. I wish I could quit dope. I'm going to delete my numbers. Right now. Okay, that's done. There's a smell in the air. It's the same smell that permeated my last apartment. Like ash and sweat. A peppery pencil smell. I can't stand it. I wonder if it's my BO or what. It must be drug-related.

One day I hope I can look back at this and really be proud of how I accomplished what I wanted to. How I brought myself back from the precipice and really pushed myself. Maybe there's some things I really need to accept that I can't change. I'll never be good at a job. Even when I was sober, I was doing shit like not showing up to work, and getting fired, and whatnot.

Okay, so I know the best thing to do is chin up and focus on the positive and PUSH myself. I pushed myself before, when I was working on the **Passions** album and was morbidly depressed but forcing myself to go into the studio every day. Maybe I can get the keys to the studio from ███████. and start working on music more regularly. Or alternatively, just bring my synths back home. I think it would be better to work out of the studio though. I'll have to bring that up with him now that he's back.

I think musically it would be good if we started playing at least once a month. Just get really good and tight. I have to convince ████████ to switch to the other drum machine he got. It just makes no sense for him to be using the synsonic, especially because his timing is inconsistent on it. I don't think he's a bad drummer I just think he needs better drum pads. The percussive possibilities that would be opened by using that thing are endless. It would really add a lot of dynamism to our sound. So, our set up would be 2 SH101s, one RS09, one urzwerg pro sequencer, ████████'s modular, the MPC, and maybe 5 or 6 pedals. Next time we meet up I'm demanding that we go to radio shack and get the adapter for the other sh101. And guitar center and get a pitch shifter and maybe another delay or reverb unit. No more sitting on our asses. And from now until April 5th we are practicing every time we get together. No more putting it off and jamming, we need to get good live, because we aren't yet. If we played tomorrow it would be an embarrassment. I want to blow everyone away at Bunker.[65] I want to show everyone up and prove how amazing we really are. I want to leave that stage and know that everyone in the audience just heard something amazing. We deserve it because we will have worked hard for it.

Gah, I'm getting worked up. J. does things I could never do in the band, that's for sure.

….I have gotten myself in way deep and I want to get out. I owe it to myself. I have so [much] potential. Maybe I truly have a mental illness and that's why I can't really succeed at life. Who knows? Maybe I'm just lazy. I do know that the way stress affects me is real, and terrible. If being successful means handling a great deal of stress, then, sadly, I'm not sure if I can be successful. Am I a fuck-up? Does a fuck-up accomplish what I have? A fuck-up accomplishes what I have and then pisses it away, like me. Or never quite manages to make it. I don't know. Who knows? Just have to get off of heroin, nothing else matters.

2.6.13

Well, that didn't work. I went from 3 stamps and ready to quit doing a whole bundle. I have to stop I HAVE to stop. Tomorrow I must not use. **Dear God, please give me the strength to not use. Please give me strength. I so desperately need it.**

I'm bored though. Took Adderall to stave off the dope cravings and of course, that was useless. So now I'm up at 4 AM wishing someone was online to talk to. And wishing I could get some sushi. At least I didn't smoke weed today? Sigh. Shakes head. Come on Ben get it together. Be the man that you should be. Be a MAN. No wonder ███████ stopped being your friend. And come on man, you know ███████ doesn't give two shits about you in the long run. I miss the summer. Aside from the fact that I didn't kiss anyone, it was a good summer. Despite the fact that I was living at home and on dope all the time. If I can get down to 2 or 3 stamps a day, then I know I can kick. I just have to have strength.

I'd like to meet a girl who, firstly, I was physically attracted to…

It could be because I don't go out. Or because I'm super picky. Or because all the women I meet have boyfriends. Who knows? Wherever I go out girls come and talk to me, I don't even need to do any work. But it hasn't gone past that…

WHAT IS WRONG WITH ME!?

I wish there were someone next to me right now. Someone I could pour my heart out to. Someone who would say, look, Ben, I will be with you as you try to get sober. I will help. I need help. Some things **I just can't do alone. I'm afraid I can't do this alone…**

I would like to meet a woman of intelligence and wit. Someone who is well-read and enjoys literature and fine art. Someone who is not a vapid nightlife scenester. Someone who dresses well or simply. Someone with good taste in music. Someone creative. Someone who sees the good in me and accepts my faults. Someone I am madly turned on by. Someone I can come home to. If I met this person, I would happily move to Park Slope with them. Start a semblance of a normal life. But I truly don't feel like I will ever meet that person. **I am 30 and I still feel as alienated and alone as I did when I was 27 or 17 or 13. Nothing has changed.** I'm still the same person. I thought 30 meant I would come to terms with myself and these things wouldn't trouble me. But I'm 30 and a heroin addict with no job prospects and dwindling musical ones.

... Anyway I'm so broken I can only go out to very specific events and not feel weird...

... But who knows, maybe I would have never made that **Passions** EP. Was all that pain and loneliness worth it? To me I guess so, I'm still very proud of that record.

How do people find the strength to do it? To get up every day and go out and hustle and work hard? I can't fucking do it. I'm not meant for NYC but I'm rich enough that it doesn't matter. But Christ what if I fuck up my inheritance. That's the only source of income I will have as I get older, and I'm starting to worry that I might waste all that money like I wasted my ▮▮▮▮▮▮▮▮▮▮▮▮ account. 60,000 on dope. 60,000. Think of all the synths, the comics, the toys, the video games, the trips overseas, everything that I could have spent that money on. I didn't even get to share being fucked up with someone else. When my parents find out the shit is going to hit the fan. I can't be on dope when that happens. I have to be able to say that I'm not using. I HAVE to. I'm no good and rotten right now. A complete wastoid. So why can't I just draw up the strength to say, hey, I don't like this, I'm going to change it. Back in the day, when I was 22 or 23 I had so much strength. And then, of course, it all burst when I entered the "real" world. **I definitely had a complete breakdown at 24.** 4 years of intense and brutal hopelessness, depression, anger, jealousy, stress so bad I was in constant agony, fear. 4 years. I don't know anyone who's been through that. Depression so pervasive that nothing you can do save sleeping can make it go away. I really don't know anyone who's suffered as badly from depression as I have. Everyone else is able to just go out and get drunk and get laid and feel good. But I can't escape how I feel, or who I am.

**Lord, please give me the strength to quit dope.
Lord, please give me the strength to quit dope.
Lord, please give me the strength to quit dope.**

2.8.13

I am so low and so alone and more than I have been in so long. I have no one to comfort me and no one to brighten my spirit or with whom I can confide. I am so low. I have nothing that I look forward to. Nothing that seems worth doing. I have no motivation and I am so unhappy. An unhappiness that visits me like a friend. A familiar feeling. Down. Deep deep down. Was I always just lying to myself about my happiness and have I forever been this profoundly alone and forsaken? **If I died today only my parents would mourn.**

2.11.13

Okay, so it's been at least a day without dope. My restless leg is absolutely killing me. I used up all my Xanax, but I think tomorrow I will call in another prescription. I've made it through the sickness but honestly, this is the worst part. My legs are so jittery. Mind over matter mind over matter mind over matter. Been taking kratom all day and I think that helps.

2.11.13

Bought four bundles. Back again. This really isn't going to end, is it? Honestly, I'm not worth saving. I look back at the last ten years of my life and the bad so far outweighs the good. I am a terrible pathetic person. Nothing but bad mistakes, hurting people, lying, being depressed, making shitty music, feeling shitty. What good have I done in my life? The **Passions** EP and Goitia Deitz and Campos Verdes and a few math head tracks. That's it. I literally cannot think of anything else that has made my life worthwhile. I haven't had a single good relationship, a single good job, I haven't been happy unless I was in complete self-delusion. **I am NOT worth saving. I am NOT worth being sober. I am such a pathetic loser.**

2.12.13

Just listened to almost all the demos I had recorded while working on the **Passions** EP. Some really good stuff. I wish I could be making as much music as I was back then. This is most likely why I feel like such a complete and utter failure. Because I am not regularly or consistently making music. I asked ███████████ to make keys for me for the studio. I will take two days a week to go in there and work on stuff and start re-recording the new **Passions** tracks. I took dope yesterday and today, but I won't take it tomorrow and then I'll see how I feel. I am still extremely low and feel empty and have no motivation to do anything whatsoever. I so dearly miss being kissed and kissing someone, and sex (good sex at least). But I can't be with anyone right now because I'm so pathetic. What do I need to do to be happy?

Quit dope. I will need to make an appointment with Dr. ███████████ and try to get a real prescription for Xanax. If I have that then I know I can beat it.

Work on music as often as possible. Two days a week for **Passions** and 1 for **Goitia Deitz**.

Work hard at school, like I used to.

Force myself to get up early every day, even if I have nothing to do, and take a walk or something. Exercise.

Travel. I need to get out of NYC.

I need help so badly. I see no future before me. I will not get married, will not have kids, will not be able to work. I am the most pathetic person I know. Listening to those old demos, at least back then I had a hunger, a drive to create, to make something worthwhile out of the desperation and hell I was going through. Now I'm too low to do even that. I make a daily schedule for myself and then I consistently am unable to follow through with it. I just want to sleep through the days. I'm afraid to go outside. It's so cold....

2.17.13

Today I really lost it. .... Something is really wrong with me, and leaving NYC is the best thing I could possibly do....

2.22.13

Thankfully I am not mourning the passing of my friendship with █████████. I just wish that I could still go to Graceland. I am going to Mexico with ██████████ on the 8th of March, so I have to be sober by then. Even if it means that three days before I go off, I need to have gotten past the sickness by the time I get there. I think it will be good tho, because I will need to be constantly doing things to keep my mind off of wanting to do dope. Going to pax will help. Maybe I can take a trip to Texas to see ██████████. Or go to Portland to see ██████████. Or London to see ██████████ and ██████████. Actually, these are all very good ideas, getting out of NYC and traveling will be super healthy for me. I had a wonderful talk with ██████████. We both talked about how much we had meant to each other, and how we will know when we are in a good relationship again.

Also had a nice little talk with ██████████ where I told her how proud I am of the songs we did together.

Endnote

65. The Bunker is a long-running bi-weekly event held at various venues in Brooklyn hosting guest DJs. thebunkerny.com/

The letter

Ben's letter, mid-February 2013:

As you can probably tell things have not been going well for me lately. As much as I try to avoid telling you when things are bad in my life, I suppose at this point I can't ignore it. I honestly hate to have to be honest with you two like this, because I really don't think either of you understand the extent of the pain that I have been living with on and off for the past decade. Nevertheless, I have literally no one else to turn to for help.

I have reached one of my worst lows, in terms of mood and functionality. I think you understand what I mean by mood: I am incredibly isolated, lonely, lack all motivation, will, or hope for improvement in certain aspects of my life in the future. In terms of functionality I mean: I cannot follow a daily schedule or routine, I cannot make myself do things that I need to do, I cannot function at the basic level of literally anyone else I know. For instance, today my plan was to get up early, go into the city and pick up my books for school, read them and go to class. I awoke at 8 AM, was unable to get out of bed until 2 PM, and then fell asleep and awoke at 9 PM.

I'd like to go on a tangent for a moment and describe perhaps my worst depressive period, and why I believe that the situation I am in right now is even worse. This period occurred between the age of 24 and 28. It began with my move to the apartment you bought me and ended when I got back on antidepressants.

During this period, I suffered a great deal. I was in such a constant state of stress that my body was in physical agony on a daily basis. I remember one time being so stressed before a show that I collapsed in the shower. When I called to tell my friends I couldn't make it because I was sick, they didn't believe me. I was suffering from hideous headaches on a weekly basis, as you may recall. What you may not know are the depths to which my depression brought me. For the entirety of this four-year period, I contemplated suicide on a daily basis (I spent the night of my 26th or 27th birthday trying to suffocate myself with a plastic bag, albeit half-heartedly). I was in such mental anguish that I would hurt myself physically: I cut myself extensively with razors and butcher knives, as well as putting lit cigarettes out on my own flesh. Sometimes I did these things in public places, in front of "friends." No one ever tried to reach out to help me. I remember after having all my things stolen while on tour in Australia I spent the night sitting on a rooftop in the rain slicing my stomach with a kitchen knife. This is the extent to which my depression affected me. I was being paid to be in Australia and given an apartment to stay in and had screaming fans who loved what I was doing and yet even amidst this depression and self-hatred found me.

I hated myself and wanted desperately to die. I had no hope whatsoever. The only thing that drove me forward was my need to create music. Somehow I managed to make it through this period and still be incredibly prolific musically. I believe music was the only thing that kept me going and kept me alive. Everything else in my life was a shambles. All my relationships during this period were loveless and painful.

With my return to therapy and then return to medication I was able to begin living a fulfilling happy life again, albeit very briefly. It was literally like a light switch had been turned on in my mind when I started taking medication again. I met ▮▮▮▮▮▮▮▮▮. I was doing well in school. I had begun to work with Jay on music that was actually enjoyable to make.

I do not understand why my natural inclination is to destroy and fuck up everything I have, but of course, before long all these things went away or were broken by myself. I failed both classes at school in order to start working at the ▮▮▮▮▮▮▮▮. I developed an extensive drug habit. At 29 I had to return home to live with you and regroup. Sadly, I didn't use this time to rebuild my life in any fashion that would provide me with a stable foundation.

Since I have moved back into the city I have physically and emotionally reached a very deep low. I have no friends to whom I can turn to for help, and I feel as if no one, utterly no one understands my situation. How can they? I don't know a single person who has lived the kind of life that I have.

Nevertheless, I am essentially friendless and loveless. I have not been with a woman in over a year. Not even kissed or been held by someone in that long.

Nevertheless, I am coming to the realization that any sort of happy relationship with someone else is so far from the realm of possibility as to be almost fantastical.

I was fired from ██████████ in December, but of course, was too ashamed to say anything. I don't think it was entirely my fault that this happened but nevertheless, it has reemphasized my uselessness. I am a 30-year-old man who cannot even hold down a part-time job at a grilled cheese shop. That is objectively one of the most pathetic things I can imagine. In fact, any objective view of myself is absolutely pathetic. I truly feel that I am broken or mentally ill or that something is not right because I am truly the most pathetic human being I know. I am unable to function at even the basest level of humanity, i.e. wake up go to work go home do it again.

Now it has come to the point where once again I can barely function. I go days and days without showering or leaving the house. The thought of doing small things like running errands almost terrifies me. I have missed almost every one of my classes so far this semester. I have not even bought any of my books. I have also, unfortunately, returned to drug use. Although I cannot emphasize enough how regardless of whether I'm on drugs or not, I am unable to hold down a job or anything like that. During my sober period (from 17 to 24) I was still getting fired from jobs and being irresponsible.

I am a broken and miserable human. Looking back at the last decade of my life fills me with regret and anger and remorse and sadness. I am overwhelmed by EVERYTHING. I truly do not understand how people can make it through day to day the way they do. I just don't have it in me to do that. I used to have a drive to, despite everything, make music, but it seems like my outlets for creativity have narrowed. I am lucky to be able to get into the studio with Jay once a week.

The very real conclusion is that I will never be able to live a truly normal productive life. I am incapable of holding down a job. I am incapable of having a healthy relationship (sad to say, I don't think I will ever be able to have children. If I can't hold down a job, how can I raise an infant?). I have an abundance of talent but not much to show for it. I am attractive and yet it's been over a year since I've been with someone. That truly is utterly pathetic.

I feel as if almost everyone I know looks down on me. I would look down on myself as well. I don't understand how I could be given so much to work with (money, talent, attractiveness), and yet be unable to make any of it work. Anyone else given my resources would be an incredible success. Instead, I am a 30-year-old man who cannot and, most likely will never be able to support myself. It saddens me to realize that I feel just as isolated and alone as I did when I was 24, 17, or 13.

Nothing has changed, I am still far away and all alone.

I wish I knew if I was just born without the faculties to operate in modern society, or if I am just lazy. I know that stress affects me more so than anyone I know (I don't know anyone who gets so stressed out driving that they break into a cold sweat and have to puke up after being in traffic).

Thusly I will never be able to succeed past a certain point, as success means dealing with stress. I will never be a successful musician or writer, sadly, because once I reach a certain level the stress becomes too much for me.

I could go on but I've exhausted myself. I don't know what to do with myself and I don't know how to fix this awful state that I'm in. I wish I could just get by without telling you any of this. I'm honestly not really sure if either of you can help me in any tangible way. I feel quite distanced from both of you, as neither of you I feel truly understands what my life is like. Or who I really am.

I can tell you at least that I will not kill myself while you are alive, so you need not worry about that.

I don't know what to do, perhaps you can help. At least this explains why I don't pick up my phone.

A day later we received an additional email. I am including a few key fragments here:

I hope that this hasn't upset either of you too much, although I'm sure it will. I feel that it is important that you know these things about me though. I am tired of hiding the amount of pain I have been through. I know that both of you love me very much and that is why I have avoided telling you any of these things. At your age, I feel like it is selfish of me putting the two of you through what I have been through. Perhaps I'm just being a baby and I need to grow up. And please understand that I recognize that I am not entirely a victim. I am not a very good person and I probably deserved most of the pain I have received in my life. I know there are certainly a great number of individuals who feel I deserve the pain I am in.

Nevertheless I don't want very much out of life, which is perhaps why it is all the more distressing to me that I am unable to function at such a basic level.

If I could [manage it], this is what my life would be like:

> I would like to have a job that I am not afraid of. It has always been difficult for me to work because I am constantly afraid of making a mistake...
>
> I would like to do something creative every day, or at least every day...
>
> I would also very much to be recognized for my work by my peers...
>
> I want to enjoy life and be excited by it. I want to look forward to things...
>
> Finally, I would like someone to share life with... Sometimes I feel like I am doomed to a life of loneliness, however. Maybe there a foulness in our family's blood, maybe we are all doomed to be unhappy...

As you can see I have a vision of what good life for myself would be like. I don't know why it has been so hard to attain even a semblance of these things...

Sometimes I feel like I am a developmentally disabled individual who needs to have a "coach" around to help me through the day to day. That is how low my opinion of myself is...

I just wanted to write this additional email so that you can see that I am not completely without hope.

— Ben

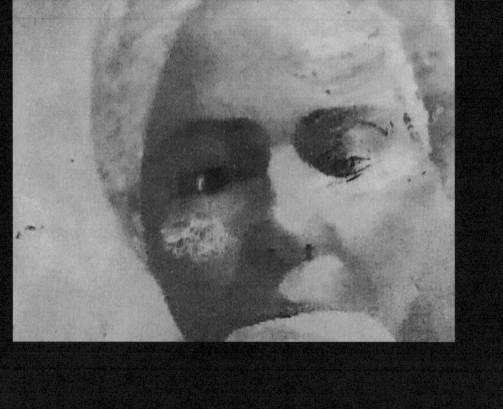

This was the first time you let us in.

Three pages were attached to an email, describing the private hell into which your life had devolved. Back then, I used to teach one semester a year in a small college in the south of Israel. The email arrived toward the middle of February 2013, while I was in Israel teaching. The time difference between Israel and New York is 7 hours, with Israel ahead, so I was the first one to read it in the morning. I immediately called Roger, who was home in Larchmont. It was 2 in the morning, New York time. I asked him to check his email and read Ben's letter to us. And so, he did.

Roger reached out to a close friend in California, a clinical psychologist with many years of experience who knew us and Ben very well. She suggested getting in touch with an outpatient program treating chemical dependency in adults, in New York City. It was considered one of the best treatment centers in the city.

Roger did not lose any time in bringing Ben home from his apartment in Brooklyn. He got in touch with the suggested program right away. Acting quickly was a must.

All that we had to count on and guide us was courage, intuition, and love for Ben. We were going to take Ben into our hands and observe the wounds of drugs, loneliness, and depression.[66]

> *We would explore his Bardo in between worlds,*
> *where he had fallen,*
> *and lead him out of valley of death.*
> *So did we all desire.*

Thus was the beginning of Ben's journey to sobriety.

Ben's journal during intensive outpatient therapy (shortly after we received his letter):

2.23.13

When I go see the doctor counselor guy on Monday, this is what I plan to tell him.

"First off, the reason I'm here is because I am not happy with where I am in life or who I am in life. I want to be a better person, and I have a clear idea of who that person is. I need help to get there but I want to get there. Basically, I want to be a good person, someone who bettered people's lives through his existence rather than worsened them. Someone who is at peace with who he is, and happy with who he is. I don't want to be a pop star and make a million dollars. I just want to be a good person who enjoys his creativity. I think I've been this person before and I can become him again. I think the first step in that direction is getting off of drugs. I don't know what the second step is but I know I need a strong foundation to work with and being on drugs won't provide that.... I hope that you can help me."

2.26.13

I've been getting that scared/tense feeling where my body becomes so stressed out my skin becomes electric. I'm worried that's how it's going be if/when I see ▮▮▮▮▮▮ again. I'll write her an apology maybe in a couple months, something small and to the point. But yeah that fear. I don't like feeling it. It's not good to feel that when I'm not in the presence of danger...

I hope I can move forward and make some progress with myself. I hope I can look myself square in the face soon. With a healthy mind and a healthy body. Moving forward.

2.26.13

I am looking forward to meeting with Dr. ▇▇▇▇▇▇ tomorrow. I
think and hope that this will be the beginning of my slow climb
back towards living a good life and being a good person. Getting off
of drugs. It will take time and hard work and perseverance. I hope
I have it in me. If I can stay sober for a month, then that will be a
wonderful accomplishment.

2.27.13

Had a really good meeting with Dr. ▇▇▇▇▇▇. We discussed ways to
get off of dope, especially considering that I'm going to Mexico soon.
My options are either to check myself into St. Luke's tomorrow or the
day after and sober up or wait until Monday when I've had practice
with Hay and gotten my haircut to do it. I'm honestly leaning towards
cutting myself off on Monday (and trying to do only one on Sunday),
getting sick on Monday Tuesday and Wednesday and then flying to LA
on Thursday. I know it's insane but as much as I want to have a few
more days of sobriety on my part when I go to LA, I also know that I
really need to go to practice, and I'd like to get a haircut to look good
for ▇▇▇▇▇▇.

I know I'm going to have to apologize to ▇▇▇▇▇▇ soon. I have
been trying to formulate the words.

I know I should not go to Mexico. It is an offense to my parents. I
wonder if I was on Xanax when I decided to go. Okay. So, What's the
plan Sam? You can either

    A) Dry out at St. Luke's starting tomorrow,

    B) dry out at home, starting tomorrow,

    C) dry out at St. Luke's starting Monday and leaving
       Wednesday night,

    D) dry out at home starting Monday.

I know what I want to do, and that is D. I want to because then I get to have my haircut on Friday and my studio time on Sunday. If I go down that road then I must step down ASAP. That means cutting down to 2 tomorrow, and then 1 till Monday. I'll probably get sick tomorrow and in fact the best plan of action is to wait until I do get sick before using. It's go time.

I have much else to deal with. School is the priority. I must email them immediately. After that and when I get back from Mexico there's continuing to stay sober and practicing for the show. Going to meetings. Going to therapy. Making art. Being kind.

I don't want to go to sleep because I don't want to face tomorrow and face telling Dr. ███████ my terrible plan and emailing new school to ask for a leave of absence. Sigh. My life is so so so fucking pathetic. But you know what I think I am taking steps to remedy this. I know, once again I'm stripping everything away and starting from scratch and using my parents to get a break. I treat them like shit, I really am an awful awful son. I feel terrible about what I've put them through. So pathetic.

I think painkillers are what helped me get through my relationship with ██████ and I wish I had had them while I was dating ██████, or maybe when I was dating ██████ actually. Sigh. I have so few happy memories. My first night with ██████. Our Maine trip. That first night with ██████ again, watching doom generation, although that's bittersweet. God I'm really having a hard time. Holy shit I seriously can't think of any more... No more happy memories. None. I can think of 6 good times in my life since high school. Every memory is tinged with depression or anxiety or fear. Even if I thought I was happy I can see now how truly unhappy I was. I suppose my bike riding in the park was a very fond memory.... So much unhappiness. Too much to recount. Is this really my life?

I have no good times. I have never had good times. I have never enjoyed myself that much. I am broken. I guess that's why I have hope. I have reached the bottom. Things can only improve, right? Maybe I can start building those memories soon. Now that I'm starting my life over from zero at thirty.

2.28.13

Well here goes my crazy plan. Taper back over the next three days. Friday Saturday and Sunday. Then go off on Monday, be sick from Monday to Wednesday, then fly to LA on Thursday. Wow. I'm nuts but who knows, maybe this will work.

3.1.13

Friday night and I have no one to go out with. I want to go to some parties, one which ███████ is djing at, she hit me up to tell me she was playing there. But I can't go alone. I can't just go there and stand in the corner. This is so pathetic. How am I 30 and have no more than two friends to ask if they want to hang out. I literally have no one else I can ask to hang out with, just ███████ and ███████. Why do I have no friends? It really upsets me and makes me sad that I can't do things I want to do because I am too afraid to do them alone, and furthermore that I have no one I can call up and ask out. Why don't I have any friends? Am I too critical? Do I suck too much?

People seem to like me when they meet me. At parties they come up and talk to me. I guess if I wasn't so afraid, I'd be able to go to a party alone. Even if I was with friends, I'd be afraid. Afraid to run into someone I don't want to see. Just afraid to be out in a bar. It makes me scared. I wonder how many opportunities or experiences I've missed out on because of fear. I could take a bunch of Xanax and hope that that helps but it's not worth me wasting them, because I need them for withdrawal. The heroin doesn't even help. If I could still get high then it would take the edge off and make me super chill and comfortable going alone I think. Or I'd just end up wanting to stay home and work on stuff. I guess I better try to get some writing done or something since I'm clearly staying in tonight. Sigh. Why don't I have friends like everyone else?

It's really crazy. I have two friends that I hang out with. It makes me want to cry. Two friends in the whole city. Even if I still had the friends that I've lost or given up on, like ███████ or ███████

or ███████. or whatever, they wouldn't want to hang out with me and go to one of these things. I guess I am just unlucky in terms of friendship. Sigh. I hate this. I just want to be able to go out and maybe meet some people or whatever. I guess there's a chance of hooking up with ████████. Whatever. Another girl I screwed up with. Add her to the epically large pile. People would be stunned to know how few girls I've been with and how many amazing chances I've squandered. I'm so pathetic. **Seriously at this point no one will mourn my passing. No one will come to my funeral. I'll die alone, unloved and unmoored. I'll have accomplished nothing of significance. No one will come to my funeral. No one will care. I am so fucking pathetic.** I wish I had friends God. I really wish I had some friends dear God please let me have friends thank you Amen. I'm going to do a bunch of heroin and see how that affects me.

Such irony: when Ben died, hundreds of his friends kept coming to our home, all of them heartbroken to have lost a true friend. But depression, trauma, and addiction distorts the lens through which we view reality.

Many words were put on Facebook, as well (as transcribed):

you visited me in my dreams last
night and I slept through my alarm
because I never wanted to wake up
I woke up and now find myself
Without you again. I have so much
To tell you
I miss you like id miss my arms
Or my legs or my soul
I love you

A last journal entry:

3.28.13

I'm a little over a week sober. I have 6 bundles hidden in my house, but I haven't touched them. Today was one of the best days I've had in a long time. I got this girl ████████'s number by telling her she was stunning and gorgeous. I made a good pun (leprechaun). Jay and I wrote a new song. Driving home from the studio the full moon hung over the city and it was beautiful. It was the first time I'd felt sort of euphoric and at peace with life in a long time. I realized I've never really felt that way on dope. All my happiest times don't involve it. I guess that's a good realization. Does that mean I won't go back once I'm done being tested? I don't know. Having those buns is like a weird safety net. But it's also a test for me, one that I'm passing so far. I would really be fucked if I used. I feel like I can drink tho, and I'd love to take this girl to angel's share. Also excited to go to leather man and get a hat.

Fear

Witnessing the process of recovery calls to mind the effort needed to make music and the various elements of composition.

Melody, rhythm, and harmony are the building blocks of and the most important components in music. The first two take upon themselves the task of fusing the loose, free and easy musical notes into one sequence or a simple melody; a harmony is expressed when individual musical tones are grouped to create a cohesive whole.

Harmony elevates single notes from the limitations of their resonance when played one at a time, from commonality or predictable tones, into various changes and depth.

At times things can get complex and more so, confused. Halting a harmony, arresting the progress and calling for a new start, all over again. Recovery could go in the same route; so many times, at the moment when steps seem to be progressing, becoming smooth and harmonious, something is going wrong, and wicked.

Everything has to stop. Sometimes a real continuation is not being able to move forward.

Everything comes to a halt, discontinuing and crashing back to its starting point, again we are thrust into the depths of agony, or even despair.

There is an immediate need for rearranging, all methods and mental practices are abandoned, however coveted. A new harmony is being asked for.

The first outpatient center in NYC did not last long. Ben had to enter a full-residency rehab in Connecticut.

Its brochure read: *"Nestled on 44 beautiful acres of rolling Connecticut countryside,* ██████████ ██████████ *Hospital is renowned for its clinical expertise, proven treatments and nurturing support. Together these elements create an environment of care in which our patients reset, recover and reconnect with their lives."*

It makes me cringe, even now, but when you are desperate, one will believe anything. Bringing our son to rehab was a great deal less about the rolling hills in Connecticut, more about defeat, fear, and anguish. As we were sitting in the general office, while Ben was interviewed and examined before his admission, we could not but keep wiping rolling tears from our eyes.

I guess we were too embarrassed to let out a long and loud holler, but it was all there, fighting to let loose.

After his inpatient treatment, Ben returned home to live with us. We gave him full support, but at times, it was like walking on fire.

A different independent outpatient treatment center was selected. Again, the formula. It had many names, many superlatives and promises it could not deliver. It called itself *"A licensed and medically supervised recovery program."* It masqueraded as a clinical foundation rooted in Dialectical Behavioral Therapy (DBT), Relational Family Therapy, Cognitive Behavioral Therapy (CBT), mindfulness-based techniques, Somatic Experiencing (SE), Eye Movement Desensitization and Reprocessing (EMDR), and psychodrama.

Returning to live at home was not a good solution. Our emotional investment in his recovery placed a mental strain on all of us, but he was not ready yet to return to his previous independent way of life. We were afraid that level of exposure would lead to caving into old habits and threaten his very survival.

After a time, the decision was made to enable Ben to live in a sober house in the city, where he could continue his recovery while keeping close in touch with us.

From Ben's journal:

When it happened, I knew it was inevitable. I hadn't had the fear. From the time I entered recovery, from outpatient through inpatient and back into outpatient again, as well as I could do the next right thing, I just did not truly feel committed. I didn't want sobriety, regardless of whether I was actively planning on relapsing or not. While I liked the sense of adulthood and maturity and independence that came along with sobriety, and the validation that I was becoming a good person, deep down the most vital driving force was not there. I knew this all along, I could feel it in the back of my brain. A sense of inauthenticity. When I entered ███████ ███ my first shares at AA were about me just desperately wanting to want sobriety. And while I became more committed to acting right, my feelings did not align with those actions. It was the validation, the need to please people, the new found independence and trust from my parents, all the external factors that kept me sober. None of it was enough.

Every cliché in recovery is true. They say you pick up right where you left off, and I did.

A switch got flipped and suddenly I was the irresponsible, immature, awful person I was so desperate to set aside. It literally took one slip for me to start acting in every way I had been so desperate to grow away from; missing appointments, missing classes, skipping out on friends, sleeping late, staying in the city when I was supposed to be home. The devolution came rapidly.

The first slip was cocaine, and then I moved on to weed, as a means of dealing with the comedown. I then smoked a few more times, for no other reason then I wanted to feel different and get out of myself. Even when every time I smoked I found myself caught in a mental ouroboros of self-flagellation, praying to god to make me stop, making all the flimsy promises I had made countless times in the past, even then it wasn't enough to make me stop. It never is. I know it's impossible for me to stop on my own.

And so the fear set in. True, utter fear, the like of which I'd never known. I discovered an all-encompassing desperation. Not just one in regard to my powerless over heroin, but overall substances. I know now that I am truly and utterly powerless. I honestly didn't believe this before, and I honestly believe that, as awful as the situation is, it took this relapse for me to realize this. I can see now the person I want to be, the person I was becoming. A person who lived by the tenets of honesty and empathy and responsibility. I was growing into an adult. To be able to see that, and see how quickly that person changed into an irresponsible, lying thief, is terrifying. And it all happened in the blink of an eye. There was no slow regression but an immediate collapse into every devious habit I was capable of.

The sickening truth is that the person I am when I am using is unworthy of being loved. I was just beginning to swoon again, to feel things for people, to dream of love, and I cut those possibilities off. Likewise when I would see friends who knew of my situation but not of the extent of my relapse (I had told most about my initial cocaine use but not about anything else) I felt, and was, a liar. I went to the movies with ██████████, my last girlfriend, last week. She had been present during my descent into opiate and heroin addiction, and I had lost her to it. I told her how scared I was, how terrified I was of slipping back into who I had been. She told me I wasn't a bad person. Even back then, she said, I was, inside, a good person. She told me to go to meetings and get a sponsor. I felt like an outsider, like something was wrong with me, like a pariah, a leper. Walking through the streets surrounded by people who couldn't fathom what I was going through and who I envied for not having to.

I fooled my parents well enough. I think they wanted desperately to believe that I was remaining sober so badly that they would accept any lie I told them. Even when it was all so obvious. When I think of my father I get an ache, an awful sadness in me derived from the pain I am causing him, albeit unbeknownst to him. It tears me up. But I don't regret what happened. I'm sure I will when the repercussions happen. Nevertheless, as I said, it felt inevitable. All I want is to arrest it before it goes too far. I suppose I was waiting for someone to call me on it, and that's why it was so easy to own up to it. I know who I want, desperately, to be. It's not the person I am when I'm using. I know also that I am an addict. I have no doubt about it. I need help.

"What will it take?" I kept interrogating myself, "to bring back this wholesome, beautiful and talented child?" How could I mend the pearl necklace that my parents gave me when I married Roger?

But it was not up to me.

I knew that I had to wait for Ben to process his internal battle, to allow his mind, heart, and body to heal. He had to allow his feelings to truly percolate and then make peace with what he found there.

Suddenly (and I don't have any explanation as to why, nor can I connect it to a specific event), it was rising from within him. Therapy, AA, and the force of Ben's will seemed to combine, to intertwine tand take him somewhere new.

All of us were able to notice it, the baby footsteps toward a new and entirely spiritual self.

A commitment emerged from deep inside. Ben took new and different steps, began to thrive, his entire heart full, (he had always been so full-hearted).

An awake Ben emerged, not the one who had been broken.

You became committed to individual, group, and family therapy; sharing your and our pain from the past. This opened the door for understanding your addiction and depression, and for sharing without reservation our own life experiences. At times, this was far from easy, and you complimented us for resiliency and spirit.

Your AA group offered more than support. They hosted a haven where shame and sharing did not create a barrier. There were no obstructions, no separation. Access to your own people was allowed—after all, you are not alone in this world—and the form of camaraderie vital to a common battle was formed.

An exchange of support took place between the new circle of friends. Amendments were made. You took a moral inventory, put it into writing. It was probably the strongest I've ever seen you, not veiling any of your past or present actions; it was written inside a school notebook.

Nothing was left out. You asked yourself:

Was I selfish?

Dishonest?

Afraid?

Was I kind and loving to others?

What could I have done better?

Have I kept something to myself which should be discussed with another person at once?

Was I kind and loving toward all?

What could I have done better?

Was I thinking of myself most of the time?

Was I of help to the men who are still sick?

And you conformed—courage and honesty prevailed. Putting it into musical words:

I will gladly take the blame
For all the hurts I made
But they will never wash away
A permanence won't degrade

Reflected in the tears you cried
You once told me how the world ends
As the bonfire burn on the river's edge

You continued the one-on-one therapy sessions with a clinical psychologist, and met with a psychiatrist to monitor your medication and once a month Vivitrol injection.

You began to excel in school. You took your medication, although I am no longer sure that taking Vivitrol was such a good idea.[67] Then again, we later found 8 untouched bottles of medication called Abilify in your apartment. I know it made you gain weight, stifled your creativity. You bought it every month, but never touched it.

We will never know.

We were so proud of your hard work dedication and commitment. And you were so grateful in return.

Mark Twain once said, "Necessity is the mother of taking chances." We must demand a termination to the shameful silence, guilt, and humiliation that one endures during addiction and depression. You yourself, my son, gave an emotional yet explanatory argument to all of this, after the death of Philip Seymour Hoffman in February of 2014. You were sober at the time.

Leila Brillson, an editor for *Refinery29* magazine was a close friend. She asked you to be interviewed about Seymour Hoffman's death, in hopes that you could shed some light on the dark life of a person using heroin. You agreed to speak with her but asked to remain anonymous.[68]

From her piece:

> We spoke to a young man who was deeply affected by the death of Philip Seymour Hoffman, not only because he loved the actor, but because he also struggled with heroin — in fact, he used the same "strain" of Ace of Spades that was found in the late actor's home.
> We asked if he could shed some light on his experience, and how it makes him feel, as a former drug user, when these tragedies come to light. Here is his story:

As told to Leila Brillson:

For the record, I did not know Philip Seymour Hoffman in any real way. But I know how he felt, and in fact, he and I both knew we received similar treatments for a similar addiction. I understood what happened to him. I understood the power-lessness he probably felt before slipping back into the habit, for what was sadly the last time. I've felt it, too, on interminable subway rides and long, painful walks to my dealer. I'm struggling to make sense of how to make sense of this to you, to the person who can't fathom how a father, or a mother, or someone with all the facets of a good life can seemingly make the choice to turn their back on those things. To choose death, rather than life.

How then, to make one understand the inconceivable? Because I want you to understand. Understand calling the electric company and telling them you have cancer so you don't have to pay your bill for another month and then spend that money on crack. Understand shooting up in the same hospital room as your newborn baby. Shame. That utter and inescapable sense of aloneness. The stories change from person to person, but the feelings stay the same. **The feeling that everyone else has it all figured it out, but something deep within you is so inherently and unbelievably wrong, and this void can't ever be filled.** Not by a dump truck full of dope or booze or crack — not that it would have stopped me from trying. Understand how a partner and father can be utterly and inescapably powerless over his addiction, in the same way, that the diabetic is powerless or the cancer patient is powerless. All I ever wanted was for someone to understand.

This feeling of broken communication and desolation must only be amplified a hundred-fold amidst the pressure and superficiality of Hollywood, something PSH struggled with immensely if interviews are to be believed.

I met the news of Hoffman's passing with the same sadness and sense of loss — and shameful sense of thankfulness — that I meet when I hear of any fellow addict's passing. The question of why I am still alive when so many others are not is haunting. I sat with the discomfort of remembrance of the isolation that addic-tion wrought upon me. The friends and lovers lost. Powerless. A single step away from the death of my heart and my soul.

So, I was asked, 'Why heroin?' The simple answer is that it's the best cure for depression and anxiety that I've ever found, after decades of furious searching. It works incredibly well, in the short term. But, the long-term dividends seem to always be the same, terrific toll. Certainly, I've found that, for those with a propensity for opiates and heroin, there are no weekend warriors. I believe this self-destructive urge stems from an inherent shame — leastways it did in myself. If I was not born with a shame in me, then I developed it very early on, and likewise developed the urge to bludgeon that shame out with drugs and alcohol. Heroin was the most effective, even when it paradoxically led me to the most shameful of places. I wound up trapped in a web, ashamed of the things I'd done to escape the shame I felt so deeply inside. Constantly on the run. You could call it a weakness, but I would call it a heightened state of awareness. So heightened that I needed to dull the senses and drown out the cacophonous pitch of life.

I had to isolate myself from as much news and ignorant Facebook postings about Hoffman's death. They made me too angry — acquaintances who said he was 'no good at being a heroin addict' to celebrities calling him stupid for hurting his family. I wanted to lash out against them. Instead, I took the time to step back and accept that I had no control over other people's ignorance about addiction. **How can I judge others for being ignorant when I was ignorant myself for so long? I thought I could stop on my own, that there was something morally bankrupt in my inability to merely man up and quit after years of daily heroin abuse.** It's a difficult reality to swallow, when one realizes one's own powerlessness. Strange, too, that it's the first step in a healing process that lasts a lifetime. All I really wanted after reading those Facebook posts and tweets about his death was for those people to understand. Imagine simply that his life was taken by a disease, as deadly as cancer or diabetes. Does that make it more palatable? Try to understand. If not, it's okay. There are a million addicts that look just like you who do understand. I'm one of them.

What didn't he do that could have done? I can only know what changes I had to make in my life after suffering a relapse myself and being lucky enough to walk away from it with my life. First off, I put my recovery first, before anything else. If there was ever a question in my mind about what the most important thing in my life was, I was left doubtless after my last relapse. Without a devotion to my own recovery, a family, a career, and a happy, healthy life would never be attainable.

Addiction never sleeps. For myself, a relapse starts long before I actually put a substance in my body. It begins when I stop being honest when I start being irresponsible when I return to the habits of the addict. It may be something as simple as taking some food from my roommate without asking. It may seem like a little thing, but to me, it's a warning sign that something is up, and I have to have my feelers out for those warning signs. When they pop up, I talk about them, I'm honest about them, and I don't hide them away in the dark recesses of my brain. I let the light in.

And I'm still trying to make sense of why I am alive and so many are not. Perhaps it is because I wake up every morning and try to choose life. I take the necessary steps that are required of me to ensure that I do not wind up choosing death. The rest just isn't up to me anymore. This death reminded me that I am never cured and that my recovery is a lifelong process. That might seem like an awful prospect to someone, but it's not. Some people need to wear glasses in order to see.

A death like this one serves as a sad reminder of how easily I could slip back into past habits, and how grateful I am for the life I get to live today, drug and alcohol-free. When I see a family today, I am moved because I know I have the capacity to be a father and a loving husband, two things that I could never have been when I was using. I can be an honest and present friend. And, most importantly, I can be of service to my fellow addict, I can help those who are still in need and suffering. Today I have purpose and integrity and willingness and I can look myself in the mirror when I shave. And I need to remind myself of these things constantly because my addiction never dies.

Most of what I have written is for those who are not afflicted with addiction. Some of you who read this, however, may be. I do not write this as an excuse, but to merely tell my story and to say that we are not alone. I would have never believed in the midst of my addiction that I would have found my way out of the darkness. I could never have imagined that I would find kinship in this world. There is help and those willing to lend it. You are not alone, and never have to be again.

A melancholy smile is on my face and a tear runs down my cheek, as I read it again and again. I am, as well, *struggling to make sense of how to make sense of this to you,* and also to myself.

On April 9, 2015,

Ben celebrated his one year of sobriety.

A few close friends,
all wearing black,
Ben's favorite color,
gathered around the small table,
raising one finger up.

Many of their hands in prayer,
they peer into the flame of one candle
on top of the cake.

On May 8,

only a handful of weeks after this celebration,
Ben lost his life.

We won almost every battle
but lost the war.

> In the aftermath,
> every possible thought
> ran through my head,
> but especially this one:
> **Was I a good mother?**

Our devastation was unspeakable.
It still is.

A few months later,
we received the coroner report,
disconnected fragments of a story,
boxes checked and lines filled
on an official white form:

1. _____

2. _____

3. _____

Endnotes

66. Idea taken from the book *Compass* by Mathias Énard (trans. Charlotte Mandell),
    New Directions, first American edition, March 28, 2017.

67. About Vivitrol – www.vivitrolhcp.com › what-is-vivitrol

Art by Chagit Deitz

It is not the end

A fishing boat is sailing on – her sails are two
All of her sailors are fast asleep.
Wind is blowing over the water,
Silently a child is strolling on the shore.
He is a small and joyless child,
Endless water is washing to the far distance…
If all her sailors don't wake up
How will the boat reach the shore?[69]

On the shoreline of a sandy beach, I am walking barefoot,
holding my shoes in my hand.
Am I on Fire Island, along the Atlantic Ocean?
Is it Long Island Sound near our home in Larchmont?
Is it the immediate and small area of sand at the edge of Coffee Pond in Maine?
A domain for young Ben to race his trucks with no interference.

Or:
Is it along the salty Mediterranean Sea in Tel-Aviv
where as a child I used to build sandcastles and watch them vanish from sight?

Water is the *New Horizon*, a landscape not vanishing from my view.
A pale *shimmer moonlight*[70] hovers above my head.
I am surrounded by the *flux* of moist air; it is hard to breath.
Clouds appear and disappear, letting me watch a *helicopter* soaring up and up,
and the pale moon comes into view again.

Is it a dream?
As I keep traveling alongside the *azure* and calm water,
I wonder about the shoreline *Mode*.
Is it between the ebb and flow?

A place of transformation and hope?
May it be the place for stability and solid ground facing the ocean.
Will it have fluidity? Be a divider or a connector?
I can recognize it as a free entrance, liminal space,
threshold for dreams and imagination.

The unexpected view arrives from afar:
"Dogit Nosat" her sails are two,
 all her sailors are absent and will not come back.
The wind is blowing *endless* water are rising
warning her passengers to hold firm onto
the edge of this small watercraft.
All of them are members of my family—from the far past to the present.
My great-great-grandparents,
their children,
My grandparents,
Tony, Oscar Henrietta, and Isidore.
My aunts and uncles, from much earlier times,
long distant cousins that I have never met,
 as well as my parents, Dan and Eve, Benjamin's grandparents
who are sitting very close to him,
they refuse to let go.
My grandmother Tony is taking a close look at Peter
her 5-year-old son.
She is holding his hand, guarding him against falling into the water.
He is so young; he is my uncle
Both are mothers that worry, not to let
their children disappear again.

All of these are real images, not borrowed from my unconscious mind, I see
them as though behind a thin tissue paper, one that exposes the linkage of a
family that had to fight for their existence, and bond more than once.

History can play a cruel game.

Away in the distance,
I wave my hands
so they will notice me.
Indeed,
they wave back recognizing me and are delighted.
The small watercraft is changing direction
and coming closer toward the shoreline,
toward me.

Closer and closer

as they approach, I keep my gaze upon all of them
trying not to blink my eyes,
as not to fail to see them even for a second.
Always, I worry about losses.
Changes always change nothing different just rearranges.

The endless water is soft and yielding,
I continue to see all of them,
Now they appear to me so nearby, clear and defined.
It is not an illusion.

I recognize that all of them are present at all times, and all spaces,
shifting their ages from young to old and in between.
A medley of different languages is heard
and all of them understand each other,
mutual understanding is being formed.

Is it a magic trick? Trying to confuse me?
Or they are speaking *In Tongues? Speaking in Code?*

Art by Chagit Deitz

They are not strangers meeting for the first time, and I am still standing by the shoreline, trying to decode all that appears in front of my eyes. Bewilderment and wonder arise from some reality unknown to me, a scene that calls into question, and baffles my mind.

Is it a miracle?
Is it magic, fantasy or a dream?
No, it is not.
I put the palm of my hands parallel to my forehead,
shading my eyes and allowing the full vista to appear.

Adopting a new position, my left foot is imprisoned
and immoveable deep into the bottomless damp pit.
It is trying to lure the rest of me to join, and *leave all things behind.*
My other foot liberated and not confined, trying to assist me to avoid constant pain, not to let my other foot become ensnared.

It is not the wind that I am hearing in the background. It's a melody tuned to perfection. It is composed by my son. Everyone in the vessel attends carefully to the composition being played.

Keep the music up, fast and hard,

they request and please do not halt the music from playing.
My left foot keeps sinking down deeper into the bottomless pit
that was dug in order to lure the rest of my body to join,
and *to leave all things behind.*

I am not ready yet to join them right now.
If the music continues to play on and on,
we will never fail to connect and see each other.

The music is getting louder and closer. A succession of notes forming a distinctive sequence. All the melodies are composed by Ben and they are coming my way. A rhythmical succession of single tones, ordered for the most part within a given key, related together as to form wholesome expressive music, having the unity of what is technically called a musical thought. It is coming my way. May it be that our attachment to the music links us together—a universal language marrying the young with the old, calling our enemies into friendship, and migrate insanity into the kingdom of mental peace.

Do not stop the music, I plead, please continue. Far from shore where I stand, I am able to send Ben some messages, questions that were understood only by us two. Ben hears me and understands all of them.

Please—play my favorite piece.

It is called "Campos Verdes;" although I never understood the significance of this name, I did not ask for any explanation.

1.	**Broken Hearts, Broken Toes**	03:45
2.	**Covered Mirrors**	05:39
3.	**About Midnight**	02:32
4.	**In Caverns On Islands**	04:16
5.	**Leaving All These Things Behind**	02:43
6.	**Rooms, Instruments, Stars**	03:42
7.	**We Are Building**	02:54
8.	**Guitaring**	01:03

Track Listing for Campos Verdes' album

"Deep within the trenches of NY, lies the world of Campos Verdes. Ben Deitz shows a magnificent ability to blend many worlds and modes into something singularly his own. [With] scores of acoustic guitars, voice samples, and synthesizer, sometimes whirring away on their own and other times sailing on a bed of drum loops, Campos Verdes is an exquisite triumph. [It's] filled with vivid memories of running across green pasture in the rain and recollection of lost love adrift at sea. 'Leaving All These Things Behind' is steeped in elegance and beauty." – FOXGLOVE

The real connection between time and space is happening right now before my eyes, becoming one.

Time is shifting forward and quickly—a different act is being played. Ben transformed at once into his mid-20s, when he was a young man—I recognize his well-built body. He is very handsome, with a head full of brown hair braided with silver and gray lines.

"take me a million times and I will shake I will shake."[71]

Later, ten tracks from his last vinyl record called Passions[72]
erupts into the air:

WRISTS

(there is a pattern it forms and breaks but the center can't hold ...)

ENDLESS

(In visions that fail
muted echoes that fade
i see your face
i hear your name
watch you disappear
a slow wave comes near
standing
waiting
so far away

it will turn to dust
it will burn away
like a fading light
in a quiet place
a body without motion or presence
my breath hangs frozen in air
grasping for some sort of essence
a structure that was never there
Tried to maintain this moment forever
But it drifts away on the tide
and slips far beyond the horizon
and sinks like the sun as it dies
these words carry but fail
we stood on stones
staring into the void
as the waves crashed below
In visions that fail
muted echoes that fade
i will see your face
i will hear your name
a million miles away upon an isolating shore
waves crashing....)

waves crash
on this shore

WRISTS
ENDLESS
SENTIMENT
COMPOSURE
ELEGIAC

OUTPUT
AMNESIA
A XI
ZERO
SILENCE

Dead
Wax
RECORDS

www.deadwaxrecords.es

All tracks written, produced, performed and mixed by Ben De...

Vocals on 'Sentiment' & 'Composure' by Ben Deitz. Vocals on 'Wrists' ; 'Endless' ; 'Output' &
Giselle M. Reiber. Vocals on 'Zero' by Akiko Matsuura.

Mastered for vinyl by Nicolás Zúñiga.

This record is dedicated to Ben Deitz, who sadly left us on May 9th, 2015.
May you rest in peace and happiness forever.

SENTIMENT

(to the ocean where you wait a solemn
body by the beach wrapped in gauze
and painted black and yet just beyond
my reach... past the wreckage and the
waste of shattered clay and concrete
tombs through the depths of it all i
looked for you ...)

COMPOSURE

The paint keeps on peeling
it runs down these walls
like a memory faded
exposing our faults

through windows now broken
bonds written in glass
all we tried to cling to
with our bare hands
we were two black eyes
that blink in the sun
a ghost of a whisper
counting to none
but i lost my composure
it all fell apart
you shudder from instinct
it ends how it starts
The surface will crumble
and what's left behind
is a worthless monument
to all our designs

ELEGIAC

you can take this all away
there is nothing left for me now
nothing but an empty shell
of who i was and what i used to be

you led me through the streets
and i didn't feel a thing
not my feet on the ground
not the air on my skin…

now i feel nothing
i just don't care
i could be anywhere
i am nowhere…

The city is endless
it's cold streets i know
now nothing else matters
now i can let go…

OUTPUT

take me somewhere else
let's just disappear
anywhere at all
anywhere but here

AMNESIA

This is the sound that it makes when it starts
This is the sound of it falling apart…

I am attempting to maintain these moments—
not to let them drift away and slip far beyond the horizon.
I know that if the music goes on, I will see your face.
I will hear your name a million miles away,
upon an isolated shore where waves are crashing.
And we will never be cease to exist together.

We climb upon all music notes
Reaching for heaven
As our heart open and allows the
Most impulsive, and natural
Voice to come out
And do the unimaginable
Freeing it loudly
To touch what no one else can see.

I have to put my shoes on,
and step away.
But it is a difficult task for me,
as a small morsel of wet sand got stuck in between my left toes.

I must get it out. Otherwise, I will never fit into my shoes.

With bare hands, I try to brush the tiny pieces away,
those that keep me from stepping and moving forward.

As I go on brushing away the small pieces of sand from my foot,
I have to station my two feet on solid ground,
allowing wisdom to enter into my mind.
It tells me that, as long as the music keeps playing on,
I will never fail to see Ben.

Will it ever comfort me? I wonder.

My shoes are already on, still some sand in my shoe—I must go.

"Two weeks away feels like the whole world should have changed,
But I'm home now, and things still look the same
I think I'll leave it 'til tomorrow to unpack,
Try to forget for one night that I'm back in my flat
On the road where the cars never stop going through the night,
To a life where I can't watch the sunset

I don't have time
I don't have time....

I've still got sand in my shoes,
And I can't shake the thought of you
I should get on, forget you
But why would I want to?
I know we said goodbye,
Anything else would have been confused
But I want to see you again"[73]

I want to see you again

I want to see you again

I want to see you again

Photograph by a friend in Maine

Endnotes

68. Taken from an interview with *Refinery29*. "Why Heroin? A Former Addict Reflects On The Death Of Philip Seymour Hoffman" by Leila Brillson; February 4, 2014.

69. Again, "Dogit Nosat" is a children's poem written in 1943 by Natan Yonatan. The lyrics were composed by Lew Aleksandrowicz Szwarc.

70. Italic (but not bold) here signifies the names of Ben's songs.

71. This is a lyric from one of Ben's songs.

72. Passions – www.deadwaxrecords.es.

73. Lyrics from LyricFind.com. "Sand in My Shoes" by Richard W Nowels, Dido Armstrong, and Rollo Armstrong. © Warner Chappell Music, Inc, Spirit Music Group.

BEN DEITZ: DISCOGRAPHY

Discography sourced from **www.discogs.com**.

Math Head, *Doom & Bass*

DJ mix, МИШКА, 2006

Drop The Lime / Math Head, *Trouble & Bass*

12" vinyl, AD AAD AT (London), 2006

Math Head, *I Like Your Poetry But I Hate Your Poems Vol. 2*

DJ mix, МИШКА, 2006

Campos Verdes, *Leaving All These Things Behind*

Self-released CD-R, limited to 100 copies, 2006

Math Head, *The Most Lethal Dance*

12" vinyl and CD, Reduced Phat, 2006

Math Head, *Dirty Deeds*

12" vinyl, Terminal Dusk, 2006

Math Head, *Against All Odds*

Digital release, Trouble & Bass Recordings, 2007

Passions, *Emergency*

12" single-sided vinyl, Kitsuné Music (France), 2007

Kitsuné Maison Compilation 4 featuring Passions "Emergency (Radio Edit)"

Kitsuné Music (France), 2007

Elemental (4) "Bleep"/ Math Head "Stagger Dub"

Split 12" vinyl single, Pitch Black (UK), 2007

Math Head, *Turn The Music Up*

12" vinyl, Palms Out Sounds, 2008

Onelove: Smash Your Stereo featuring Passions "Emergency (Radio Edit)"

Sony BMG Music, 2008

San Serac, *Professional EP* featuring "Love Tactics (Passions Remix)"

Good And Evil Music (Japan), 2008

Math Head, *Stab City*

12" vinyl, Ad Noiseam (Germany), 2009

Onelove Volume 10 – Mobile Disco 2009 featuring Math Head "Turn The Music Up"

Sony BMG Music, 2009

Azure featuring Math Head, "Jambox"

12" vinyl EP, Terminal Dusk, 2009

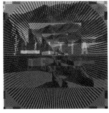

Passions, *Music Without Tears*

DJ mix, МИШКА, 2009

Goitia Deitz, *Romance / Coma*

7" 45rpm single, DiscError Recordings (London), 2011

Goitia Deitz, *Helicopter / Forever*

7" 45rpm single, DiscError Recordings (London), 2012

Goitia Deitz, *Dream Meridian*

12" EP, Cut Mistake Music, 2013

Goitia Deitz, *MODE*

12" EP, Cut Mistake Music, 2015

Passions, *Passions*

12" vinyl, Dead Wax Records (Spain), 2015

Occult Box featuring Passions "Zero"

CD boxed set, Cleopatra Records, 2015

Default Genders, *Main Pop Girl 2019*

"Pharmacoma" featuring Ben Deitz

Listen to Ben's music:

passions.bandcamp.com

soundcloud.com/goitia-deitz

Acknowledgments

Roger, you deserve special thanks for enabling me to express my own voice and for your unconditional support, patience, and endurance beyond any conventional demand.

Jaimee Garbacik (**Footnote Editorial**), my editor and friend who went to extraordinary lengths to carefully guide me and provide me with courage in this emotional journey.

Dr. Hadas Kotek, my cousin and a brilliant linguist, thank you so much for taking the time to read and review the text, always offering exceptional advice.

Bruce Rutledge (**Chin Music Press**), my publisher, for taking upon himself the task of publishing this unconventional book, as well as his generosity, wisdom, and kindness.

Dan D Shafer (**Dandy Co.**), my graphic designer who worked vigorously to improve the design and aesthetic of the project, capturing Ben's individuality as a person and artist.

All of you, my words of thanks could hardly express my feelings and sentiment.

Our family, friends, and Ben's friends, my recognition and gratitude for your love and caring.

Chagit Dietz lives in Larchmont, NY, with her husband, Roger.